"It is so good to see more and more Christians waking up to the fact that we're at war with Satan. Larry Richards is the latest to apply his considerable talents to helping us understand this war and what to do about it. May God bless Larry and the influence of this book."

Charles Kraft, professor emeritus, School of
Intercultural Studies, Fuller Theological Seminary;
author, *Two Hours to Freedom* and *I Give You Authority*

"Larry is a truly amazing gift to the Bride of Christ. His expertise and depth of wisdom concerning spiritual warfare are solidly biblical and profoundly practical. Read this book from cover to cover and then pass along these transforming truths. Larry's not a afraid to ponder the ways of the deceiver, because of his absolute confidence in our Savior."

Karl Clauson, morning host,
Moody Radio Chicago

"Larry Richards always covers a topic like *Spiritual Warfare Jesus' Way* with an in-depth Bible study. Very few are qualified to cover this subject."

Herman Bailey, host, *It's Time*

SPIRITUAL
WARFARE
JESUS'
WAY

SPIRITUAL
WARFARE
JESUS'
WAY

HOW TO CONQUER EVIL SPIRITS
AND LIVE VICTORIOUSLY

LARRY RICHARDS, PH.D.

Chosen

a division of Baker Publishing Group
Minneapolis, Minnesota

© 2014 by Lawrence O. Richards

Published by Chosen Books
11400 Hampshire Avenue South
Bloomington, Minnesota 55438
www.chosenbooks.com

Chosen Books is a division of
Baker Publishing Group, Grand Rapids, Michigan

Printed in the United States of America

Library of Congress Cataloging-in-Publication Data
Richards, Larry.
    Spiritual warfare Jesus' way : how to conquer evil spirits and live victoriously / Larry Richards.
        pages cm
    Includes index.
    Summary: "Bestselling author and respected scholar Larry Richards offers an easy-to-follow, practical, and balanced approach to spiritual warfare based on a study of how Jesus did it"— Provided by publisher.
    ISBN 978-0-8007-9585-6 (pbk. : alk. paper)
    1. Spiritual warfare. 2. Jesus Christ—Example. I. Title.
BV4509.5.R487 2014
235'.4—dc23   2014012944

Cover design by Kirk DouPonce, DogEared Design

14 15 16 17 18 19 20   7 6 5 4 3 2 1

Contents

7

Contents

Preface

Spiritual warfare is a complex and often overlooked aspect of our Christian faith. Yet the Bible teaches that a spiritual universe exists alongside the material universe, and that beings from the spiritual universe have an impact on our lives. This is clearly expressed in Paul's letter to the Ephesians. He teaches that our struggle is not against flesh and blood, but "against the rulers, against the authorities, against the powers of this dark world and against the spiritual forces of evil in the heavenly realms" (Ephesians 6:12). In Ephesians, Paul reveals the resources God provides to enable us to "stand against the devil's schemes" (6:11). My book on Ephesians, *The Full Armor of God* (Chosen, 2013), is about how we defend ourselves from attacks mounted by Satan and his demons.

In this book we look at Jesus' confrontations with Satan and evil spirits, and find principles that can guide us whenever we are called upon to aid a person suffering from demonization. We will also learn about general combat for the day-to-day warfare with demons that every believer faces. In the appendix we look at, and comment on, every reference in the gospels to Christ's conflict with evil spirits. In the process we will learn how we can be instruments of God's redemptive grace, and continue Christ's ministry of setting Satan's captives—ourselves included—free.

Raleigh, North Carolina
October 2013

Part 1

Roots of the Invisible War

1

The Stranger

As the first book of the Bible opens, God shapes a world as a home for humankind. He fills this world with beauty and with living creatures, which He calls "good." He regulates the course of the stars in the heavens. He patterns day and night, with season following season, to provide the world with stability and security. And then God creates human beings in His own "image" and "likeness" (Genesis 1:26).

It is clear in the Genesis account that God created us in His image so that He might love us and that we might return His love. Animal life is "good," but after creating humans God pronounced His handiwork "very good." And God sought out the first humans in a Garden He designed for their delight, to walk and talk with them.

The picture drawn in Genesis 1 and 2 is one of God and humans sharing an essential likeness, taking delight in each other. This picture reminds us that the Bible basically tells a love story. Scripture is about the relationship between the Creator and unique creatures He fashioned with the capacity to know and to love Him, even as He knows and loves us.

But the idyllic vision of early Genesis is soon shattered. A stranger appears, hosted in the body of a serpent, whose intent is to drive a wedge between God and human; to distort and destroy the love relationship that existed at the beginning.

We all know who the enemy is from our Sunday school days. Even children understand that the serpent represents God's enemy, Satan. Even children understand that Satan succeeded in alienating human beings from the Creator. As an early American primer for schoolchildren rhymed, "In Adam's fall/we sinned all."

The problem with the Sunday school approach, however, is that the treatment of the story—while factually accurate—is superficial. There are significant issues raised in early Genesis that we tend to ignore.

Genesis 1, for instance, usually is taken as a description of the original creation of the universe. The account of each day's work describes what God did to fashion the heavenly bodies and the planet that is our home. But there is no mention of the stranger's creation in a single one of the seven days. So where did Satan come from? And when did Satan come?

Answers to these questions provide important insights into the nature of an invisible war that is still being waged in a dimension that is largely hidden from our view. Yet one thing is clear from the Genesis account: Wherever Satan came from and whenever he came, this being has an impact on our world.

Later in the Genesis story, Adam and Eve are driven from the Garden that God fashioned for them. At that time God places something called "cherubim" on the east side of the Garden "to guard the way to the tree of life" (Genesis 3:24). Commentators differ on the mission of the cherubim. Were they placed there to keep Adam and Eve from returning to the Garden? Or were they placed there to keep Satan from closing off forever the possibility of endless life for human beings?

Whatever the reason, early Genesis speaks of a stranger who succeeds in alienating Adam and Eve from the Creator. Early Genesis also identifies another kind of being, cherubim, armed with a flaming sword and charged with guarding the way to the Tree of Life.

Again, any Sunday school student can identify both the stranger and the cherubim. Ask a child, and she will tell you that the first is a "bad angel" and the second is a "good angel." But even her teacher is unlikely to notice that neither of these beings is mentioned in the Creation account. Even the teacher is unlikely to see the significance of their appearance here, in the opening chapters of the book of Genesis. Yet their appearance here truly is significant. The appearance of Satan and the cherubim tells us that there is a dimension beyond our own, and that beings from this dimension can enter our world. And it tells us that these beings can impact you and me in what we too often think of as the "real world."

What is more, early Genesis tells us much about the stranger and about what is happening in this other dimension, a dimension we often call the spiritual world, but which the apostle Paul calls "the heavenly realms" (Ephesians 6:12). What does Genesis tell us? First, that there is at least one being in the spiritual world who is the enemy of the Creator. He is filled with animosity for the Creator and is determined to do everything he can to disrupt God's plan for human beings. This enemy is intent on turning these creatures God loves against Him, and on twisting their love for Him into fear.

Second, the flaming sword held by the cherubim tells us that God has His supporters in the spiritual realm. It also indicates that there is active warfare going on there between

Satan, with any forces he might have, and the Creator, with the angels who are committed to His cause.

And once again, we are shown that this war between God and Satan, although conducted in a spiritual realm to which we have no access, can and does have an impact on us in our world.

In a moment we will look more closely at the stranger, Satan, to discover his origin and motives. And we will look more closely at his followers, for Satan does have followers. But for now it is enough to recognize that a spiritual world, populated by beings who are at war with each other, is revealed in the earliest chapters of the Word of God. And it is enough to see in these early chapters of Genesis that the war is not fought in the heavenlies alone. Earth, too, is a battlefield. Even as the forces of evil corrupted Adam and Eve, so Satan's forces seek to corrupt human beings today.

What is so exciting to me in writing this book is the realization that you and I are not simply spectators (or victims) of this invisible war. God has called and equipped us to be warriors. And as spiritual warriors we can conquer evil spirits when they attack us and our fellow human beings.

As we read deeper into this book we will learn how to conduct spiritual warfare Jesus' way, to set others, and ourselves, free.

2

The Other "Beginning"

In the ancient land of Uz, a good man named Job is suffering. He has lived his entire life dedicated to doing what he believes is right (see Job 31). But then Job experiences sudden, devastating reverses. In a single day his wealth is taken from him, and his sons and daughters are killed. A short time later, Job is afflicted by agonizing sores that break out all over his body.

Job, along with several friends, struggles to understand these terrible happenings. They simply cannot be dismissed as coincidences. What, they wonder, has Job done to deserve all this pain?

Job is the most puzzled of all. His friends agree that, since God is always fair, Job must have committed some secret sin. But Job's conscience is clear. Examining his life carefully, Job can find no flaw that might have exposed him to such terrible judgments. Perhaps the greatest hurt of all is Job's growing conviction that what has happened to him is unfair. Job has done nothing wrong. Yet God, who Job has always assumed blesses the righteous and punishes the sinner, is not being fair to him.

It is only near the end of the Bible's book of Job that God answers him. In some ways, the answer seems unsatisfactory. God's simply confronts Job with His omnipotence and His wisdom. Who, then, is Job to judge the Creator's ways? The Lord's first words to Job are about Creation. And within this poetic dialogue, God provides a startling revelation:

> "Where were you when I laid the earth's foundation?
> Tell me, if you understand.
> Who marked off its dimensions? Surely you know!
> Who stretched a measuring line across it?
> On what were its footings set,
>   or who laid its cornerstone—
> while the morning stars sang together
> and all the angels shouted for joy?"
>
> Job 38:4–7

It is these last two lines that are startling. Hebrew poetry relies on parallelism and repetition of thoughts. These lines unmistakably portray "morning stars," angels, celebrating joyfully as they witness the creation of our earth.

We will return to God's dialogue with Job and what is revealed to him, but let's shift our thoughts for a moment to the obvious point being made here involving Creation: The spiritual universe and its inhabitants were created *before* the material universe. The spiritual universe was already populated by beings we know as angels. And by the stranger, Satan, and those who chose to become his followers.

What Happened before Genesis?

What happened in the spiritual universe long before the events described in Genesis 1? We know that God populated that universe with living beings, even as later He would populate ours. But just as things seem to have gone wrong in our universe, where Adam and Eve chose independence over allegiance to the Creator, things went wrong in the spiritual universe as well.

What happened is described in two of the Bible's books of prophecy. Ezekiel is prophesying against a prince of Tyre, when unexpectedly he focuses on another being, a "king of Tyre." This king is not human, but is described as a "guardian cherub" (Ezekiel 28:14). The text tells us, "You were blameless in your ways from the day you were created till wickedness was found in you" (verse 15). God, speaking through the prophet, goes on to remind the "guardian cherub" that because of that wickedness "I drove you in disgrace from the mount of God" (verse 16).

But what was the wickedness that caused this mighty angel to be expelled from God's presence? The answer is found in Isaiah 14, where the thoughts and intent of this particular morning star are revealed.

"I will ascend to heaven; I will raise my throne above the stars of God; I will sit enthroned on the mount of assembly, on the utmost heights of the sacred mountain. I will ascend above the tops of the clouds; I will make myself like the Most High."

Isaiah 14:13–14

Simply put, the guardian angel was not satisfied with the role he was created for. The "I will" statements reveal his intent to push God from the throne of the universe and take the Creator's place.

But God responded to the challenge, and the text reminds the great fallen angel of God's action. "How you have fallen from heaven," Isaiah says, "O morning star, son of the dawn! You have been cast down to the earth" (Isaiah 14:12).

And here, cast down but still powerful, the rebel angel became Satan, a jealous and implacable enemy of the God who created him.

God's Enemy—and Ours

It is no surprise that "Morning Star," now Satan, is the enemy of God, or that he is eager to attack those of us who are committed to the Lord. Something that we can see, but that Job cannot, is that Satan has a critical role in Job's suffering. In the opening chapters of the book that tells Job's story, Satan is complaining that God has erected a hedge of protection around the blameless Job. Remove that hedge, Satan challenges, and Satan will make Job deny God to his face. It is then that the series of disasters orchestrated by Satan strikes the innocent Job. And when Satan's first efforts fall short, God gives Satan permission to attack Job directly. But even the painful boils that cover Job's body do not move Job to repudiate God. Yet these terrible experiences do create doubts, and undermine the image of God that has always sustained Job.

It is fascinating that by the end of chapter 2 of the book of Job, Satan skulks offstage, a humiliated failure. But the story of Job's struggle to reconcile his sufferings with his understanding of God continues, chapter after chapter. It is only after God speaks directly to Job, not to answer Job's questions but to reveal Himself, that Job is satisfied. "My ears had heard of you," Job says, "but now my eyes have seen you. Therefore I despise myself and repent in dust and ashes" (Job 42:5–6). Job no longer will question God's wisdom or His goodness. Job will simply trust the God who has revealed Himself through the suffering Job has experienced.

Questioning God

It is something we just cannot seem to help doing. There are so many questions we desperately want answered. Perhaps most compelling of them is, Why did God permit Satan to rebel? We also wonder, Why does God permit good people like Job to be attacked by Satan? And, Why did God let Adam and Eve declare independence and bring so much suffering on their descendants?

We cannot answer these questions fully. But we are forced to notice that God gave both humans and angels a free will. Humans, and angels as well, were created with the ability to choose. When we look back at Genesis 1 and 2, and see the love that motivated the creation of our race, we can at least begin to understand.

God created human beings as persons whom He could love and be loved by in return. But for love to be real, it must be given freely. We might pay a person to act as though he or she loves us. Or we might coerce a person by force to pretend to love us. But real love, true love, must be given freely and spontaneously.

If love truly is important to God—and the gift of God's Son as a sacrifice for our sins reveals how important love is to the Creator—then God simply had to create beings who were free to love Him and were just as free to turn away from Him.

That is the choice that the guardian angel known as Morning Star made. Rather than return God's love, he chose to challenge God for supremacy in God's universe, and he was thrown down.

Whatever love the guardian angel might once have felt for his Creator turned to an implacable hatred, and he became Satan. Even worse, the Bible indicates that perhaps as many as a third of the angels chose to rebel with Satan (see Revelation

12:4) and became Satan's "angels" (Matthew 25:41), known today as evil spirits or demons. And because Satan and his followers hate God, they are also enemies of humans, and especially of those of us who follow Jesus. They are intent on harming us, even as Satan's blows caused Job to suffer.

We must know not only how to defend ourselves, but also how to set Satan's captives free.

3

Behind the Curtain

The book of Job pulls back the curtain that separates the material from the spiritual universe. In Job we catch a glimpse both of God and of His great adversary, Satan, and gain insight into the nature of the war they are waging. It is important not to misunderstand what we are shown.

We are told, "One day the angels came to present themselves before the LORD, and Satan also came with them" (Job 1:6). There is no question from this text that the Lord is supreme. All the angels, including Satan, are inferior to Him.

We are told that the Lord asks Satan if he has "considered" Job, and God goes on to describe him as "blameless and upright, a man who fears God and shuns evil" (1:8). Satan surely has considered Job. In fact, Satan has tried to get at him! But Satan complains, "Have you not put a hedge around him and his household and everything he has?" (1:10). Clearly, God can provide for and protect His own. Satan cannot break through the barriers that God has erected.

So Satan argues that Job's behavior is rooted in self-interest. Job does not really care about God; he just wants the good life that God has provided for him. Satan challenges God: "Stretch out your hand and strike everything he has, and he will surely curse you to your face" (1:11). Again the implications are clear. Satan is determined to alienate Job from God, and cause Job to repudiate the Lord.

The Lord then removes His protection, saying to Satan, "Very well, then, everything he has is in your hands" (1:12). While Satan's motives are clear, God's motive in permitting Satan to attack Job is not clear. Some have seen this simply as a contest, with Job a mere pawn in a cosmic game played by God and Satan. But this view ignores a reality confirmed throughout Scripture. God loves human beings. He does not "use" us.

Satan then devises and causes the disasters that strip Job of his possessions and of his children as well. The pure evil and wickedness of Satan are clearly revealed.

Despite what Satan has done, rather than curse God, Job "fell to the ground in worship" (1:20).

Satan is not ready to give up, and insists, "Skin for skin! . . . A man will give all he has for his own life" (2:4). God removes another barrier, and Satan afflicts Job with painful sores "from the soles of his feet to the top of his head" (2:7). But again Job refuses to curse God, saying, "Shall we accept good from God, and not trouble?" (2:10).

It is at this point that Satan slinks offstage. He has utterly failed in his attempt to alienate Job from the Creator.

The Story Continues

But the story of Job does not end here. The book of Job continues for forty more chapters! Again, Satan's motives for attacking Job are clear, but we do not yet understand God's reason for permitting Satan to torment this good man.

I believe the key to understanding God's intent is found in Job's words recorded in Job 3:25, and in his later admission in Job 42:5, which we will look at in a moment. As Job shares his doubts and fears with his three friends, he says, "What I feared has come upon me; what I dreaded has happened to me" (3:25).

Yes, Job is a blameless and good man "who fears [respects] God and shuns evil" (1:8). But in Job's view, God is a judge who goes strictly by the book. Job believes that the blessings he has enjoyed are blessings earned by his good works. And Job is afraid that he simply cannot continue to be good enough to retain God's favor. So when the disasters strike, Job blurts out, "What I dreaded has happened to me."

But under the probing of three of his friends, Job finds himself defending his righteousness. Nothing he has done merits the disasters that have befallen him. God actually *is* being unfair! And Job's concept of God and of relationship with Him is shattered.

As the book ends, God reveals Himself to Job. He does not explain why He permitted Satan to carry out the attacks. Satan's part is never mentioned. God simply gives Job a glimpse of His power and His wisdom, and in that revelation He invites Job to trust Him. And Job does! "My ears had heard of you," Job says, "but now my eyes have seen you" (42:5). Job has experienced the presence of God and no longer questions or doubts.

God affirms the rightness of all of Job's questionings. And, the text tells us, "The LORD blessed the latter part of Job's life more than the first" (42:12).

Insights into the Invisible

Job is one book in the Bible that draws back the curtain and lets us gaze into the spiritual world that exists alongside our own world. And Job gives us insight into the nature of the invisible war that is going on between God and Satan today. In Job we learn that Satan intends to strike at God by continuing to try to alienate us from the Lord, even as he alienated Adam and Eve.

In Job we learn that Satan, although he has free will and exercised it to plot the disasters that struck Job, is still subject to his Creator. God is able to thwart Satan's efforts and set up barriers that Satan cannot pass.

In Job we learn that Satan is fully capable of manipulating events in the physical universe. Satan can affect our circumstances and influence us as we live our lives in this world.

In Job we learn that Satan has no regard for human beings, and may even delight in doing us harm.

And in Job we learn that, while Satan may seem to succeed in attacks on human beings, his efforts ultimately fail to accomplish what he sets out to do.

We also learn important things about God. In Job we are reminded that God is sovereign, and every being in the spiritual universe is subject to Him. Satan may be powerful, but God is all-powerful.

In Job we learn that God might permit Satan's attacks on His people, but in the end what Satan does will accomplish God's purposes, not the devil's.

In Job we learn that our personal relationship with the Lord is of supreme importance to Him. He loves us for ourselves, not for what we do. As determined as Satan is to alienate humans from God, the Lord is just as determined to draw humans to Himself. This goal is so important to Him that

God may permit us to suffer under Satan's attacks, if that is what it takes to deepen our relationship with Him.

Perhaps most important, we see that the invisible war is really all about us. We are important to the God who loves us, in and of ourselves. We are even important to Satan, but only as means by which he can strike out at the God he hates. The one could not care less about us. The Other loves us so much that He gave His Son that we might have everlasting life (see John 3:16).

And the story of Job reminds us that there is no way we can avoid entanglement in the invisible war that is going on between God and Satan, between angels and demons. Satan will strike at us, however innocent we may be, in order to get at God.

But today we are not called to stand by helplessly and simply suffer the attacks of Satan's evil spirits. We are called to be actively engaged in the struggle as God's warriors. And God has equipped us to overcome the demons who oppress us and others today.

We are called to engage in spiritual warfare Jesus' way.

4

A New Phase Begins

With the appearance of Jesus a new phase of the invisible war began. With the exception of a few passages, like those in Job 1 and 2, the impact of the spirit world on lives in our world has been more or less hidden. As Christ began His earthly ministry, evil spirits were confronted, and what had been an invisible form of warfare became open and public.

It is not that humans have been entirely ignorant of the existence of an invisible war. Every culture has stories of ghosts and spirits who act on humans, usually to cause harm. Most cultures have witchdoctors or *shamans*, whose task it is to protect people from evil spirits or to manipulate the spirits into providing benefits. In nearly every culture the entities that populate the spirit world are viewed with fear. But in no culture are the medicine men seen as more powerful than the spirits they deal with.

In first-century Judea, the homeland of the Jews, people were fully aware that evil spirits existed. Evil spirits and demons were often held responsible for illnesses and other personal disasters. The Jews even had individuals who presented themselves as exorcists, who promised to drive out demons for a price. These Jewish exorcists claimed no power or authority over evil spirits, but relied on occult incantations and formulae to chase demons away.

Alfred Edersheim, in his *Life and Times of Jesus the Messiah* (Eerdmans, 1967), records a simple incantation recited by Jewish exorcists when attempting to drive out demons: *Burst, curst, dashed, banned be Bar-Tit, Bar-Tima. Bar-Tina, Chashmagoz, Merigox, and Isteaham.*

We can imagine how effective such incantations were against what the apostle Paul calls "spiritual forces of evil" (Ephesians 6:12)! And we can understand the amazement of a congregation meeting in a Capernaum synagogue when an evil spirit disrupted the service. Mark describes what happened next:

> "Be quiet!" said Jesus sternly. "Come out of him!" The evil spirit shook the man violently and came out of him with a shriek. The people were all so amazed that they asked each other, "What is this? A new teaching—and with authority! He even gives orders to evil spirits and they obey him."
>
> Mark 1:25–27

Truly it was a new teaching. A new day had dawned for humanity. Jesus had—and has!—authority to "give orders to evil spirits," and they must obey.

Jesus did not rely on incantations. He recited no magical or semi-magical formulae. Jesus simply commanded. Satan's fallen angels, which the New Testament calls "demons" and "evil spirits," were forced to obey.

What about Us?

Later as we follow Jesus through the gospel records, we come across something even more amazing: Jesus commissioned His twelve disciples and "gave them authority to drive out evil spirits" (Matthew 10:1; see also Mark 6:7). Christ's power over evil spirits was so complete that He was able to give His apostles authority to drive them out in His name.

Luke tells us of another time when Jesus appointed 72 of those with Him to go on a preaching mission throughout Judea. The 72 were not apostles, but simply followers of Jesus. In instructing them Jesus did not explicitly grant them power over demons. Yet when the 72 returned, they were filled with joy and reported, "Lord, even the demons submit to us in your name" (Luke 10:17). Even ordinary followers of Christ were able to command evil spirits in Jesus' name. And the demons were forced to submit.

Followers of Jesus would no longer be helpless victims of evil spiritual forces at war with God. Instead, ordinary followers of Christ would be able to conquer evil spirits. And this would be done in Jesus' name, with total reliance on His power and His authority.

Another Mission?

We are used to thinking of the mission Jesus undertook in coming to earth in terms of John 3:16. "For God so loved the world that he gave his one and only Son, that whoever believes in him shall not perish but have eternal life." And we should see Jesus' incarnation, His death on the cross and His resurrection as redemptive. Christ paid the penalty for our sins, winning full and complete forgiveness for us. In

His resurrection He infused eternal life into us who were spiritually dead. And with that new life, Jesus brought us into God's family as adopted sons and daughters (see Ephesians 1:5). In this, God "rescued us from the dominion of darkness and brought us into the kingdom of the Son he loves" (Colossians 1:13). Considering what Jesus has done for us, it is appropriate that we respond with praise and thanksgiving.

But there is another purpose God intends to achieve through the incarnation, death and resurrection of Jesus. The apostle John states that purpose clearly in his first epistle: "The reason the Son of God appeared was to destroy the devil's work" (1 John 3:8).

That Greek word translated "destroy" here is *lyo*. It means "to undo." The broader thought here is that Satan, who controls human cultures and societies (see 1 John 5:19), has constructed a kingdom of evil (see Ephesians 2:1–3), in which he holds humans captive (see 2 Corinthians 4:4). Jesus came not only to redeem us, but also to tear down the kingdom of evil that Satan has constructed.

John's statement of God's intent to "destroy the devil's work" has direct application to offensive spiritual warfare. Wherever Satan's demons gain a foothold in a person's life, we are confronted with "the devil's work." And using the authority Jesus gives us, we are to confront evil spirits and drive them out. In this way we participate in Christ's destruction—His undoing—of the devil's work.

It is no surprise, when we see our mission as one of conquering evil spirits, that Satan has worked industriously to blind believers to the reality of spiritual warfare. He is desperate to keep Christians ignorant of the authority we have to confront and to conquer evil.

The invisible war is a real war, and it is going on today. And demons do look for any access to cripple believers—sometimes physically, certainly emotionally and often psychologically. What a joy it is to discover that we ourselves can confront and can conquer evil spirits when we conduct spiritual warfare against them Jesus' way!

Summary of Part 1

Roots of the Invisible War

The first two chapters of Genesis reveal the existence of an invisible war and the existence of a stranger who is intent on alienating human beings from the God who loves them. The origin and motivation of this being, whom we call Satan, is described in Isaiah 14 and Ezekiel 28.

A powerful angel, one of the cherubim, determined arrogantly to supplant the Creator, rebelled and was supported by a number of other angels. The result was a resounding defeat for Satan and his followers. But they continue their war against God and continue to try to alienate humans from the God who loves them. In the book of Job, we see one incident in this continuing warfare, in which Satan attempts to get a man named Job to curse God. Despite the suffering that Satan inflicts on Job, Job will not repudiate his Creator. Satan has failed in his purpose. But God has had a hidden purpose in permitting Satan to torment Job. Through the experience, Job comes to know and trust God fully, and the end of his life is filled with blessings.

The story of Job illustrates the implacable hatred Satan has for God and his utter disregard for the pain he causes human beings. The story also illustrates the fact that God is able to turn what Satan intends for evil into something that will benefit the sufferer. Yet in this story we see that Job is essentially powerless, a victim of the warfare going on around him.

With the incarnation of Jesus, momentum in the war shifts. Jesus confronts and drives out the evil spirits who are tormenting humans, and He even gives authority to His followers to repel evil spirits in His name. In mounting offensive attacks on the demons who torment human beings, first Jesus, and then you and I as His followers, have begun to dismantle the kingdom of evil Satan has been building in our world. In confronting and conquering evil spirits, we join Jesus in destroying the devil's work.

Part 2

Personal Preparation

5

Adam's Flaw

Adam stood beside Eve in the Garden, listening to the words of the serpent that hosted Satan. The serpent's suggestions were subtly cast to undermine the first pair's relationship with God.

"Did God really say . . . ?"
"You will not surely die!"
"You'll be like God, knowing good and evil."

Eve pondered the serpent's words. The fruit was pleasing to the eye. It was fragrant, good for food. And besides, it was desirable for gaining wisdom. And so she ate, and gave some to her husband.

Adam took the fruit from her hands and ate also. The Bible later says, "Adam was not the one deceived" (1 Timothy 2:14). The serpent had fooled Eve. But Adam was fully aware of the nature of his choice.

The Last Adam?

It may seem strange to think of Jesus as the "last Adam." But this is just how Scripture casts Him. In 1 Corinthians 15:45, Paul paraphrases Genesis 2:7: "The first man Adam became a living being," and then adds "the last Adam, a life-giving spirit."

There are so many contrasts and comparisons that can be drawn between Adam and Christ. Each entered the world as an innocent, free from sin. Each represents a new beginning. And each was approached by Satan, in an attempt to alienate him from the Father.

As we consider our calling to confront evil spirits and conduct spiritual warfare Jesus' way, there is much to learn from the temptation of Christ. Jesus was about to set out on the mission for which He had come into our world. And, as strange as it may seem, it was necessary for Jesus to demonstrate that He was personally fit to undertake that mission.

Jesus was certainly qualified to answer the call. Matthew's gospel focuses on His qualifications. Jesus was a descendant of David, qualified to fulfill the Old Testament's predictions of a messianic ruler. Matthew emphasizes Jesus' virgin birth, reports on the visit of the Magi who saw His star appear, and tells of His escape to Egypt and return to settle in Bethlehem. Matthew documents each event as a fulfillment of biblical prophecy. Matthew goes on to report the testimony of John the Baptist, and to quote God as saying, "This is my Son, whom I love" (Matthew 3:17).

Jesus was ready to step into history and complete the mission on which He was sent!

Yet it was at this point that Jesus was "led by the Spirit into the desert to be tempted by the devil" (Matthew 4:1). Note the implications. God's Spirit led Jesus into the desert, one of the most desolate places on earth. There Jesus would wait, without food, seared by the sun, panting in the stifling heat. And the express purpose for God's leading Jesus into the desert was that He might "be tempted by the devil." Jesus was qualified as both Messiah and Savior. But was Jesus, *as a human being*, able to meet Satan's challenge? I know this seems like a peculiar question. And yet it is an important one. Adam, for all his advantages, abandoned total allegiance to his Creator. If Jesus was to be the last Adam, the "second man" (1 Corinthians 15:47), bringing life to those Adam doomed to death, He needed to demonstrate the commitment that the first Adam had failed to show.

The Dangers of Distractions

This is an important question for you and me to ask ourselves as we realize that Jesus has given us authority over evil spirits. Are we really able to meet Satan's challenge? You and I as believers in Jesus are qualified. We have been adopted into God's family. We have been given new life and have been infused with the Holy Spirit. And Jesus has given us authority. We are qualified to conquer evil spirits. But whether or not we are able to meet and defeat Satan's minions rests on whether or not we are truly committed to Jesus, and whether or not our confidence is truly in the Lord.

That is why in the next three chapters we will look closely at the temptation of Jesus. We will examine the strategies Satan used in his attempt to distract Jesus from His mission— strategies Satan might use in an attempt to distract us and make us impotent in spiritual warfare. But first, let's briefly review the strategies Satan used in his successful attempt to turn the hearts of Adam and Eve.

"Did God Really Say . . . ?"

Satan asked, "Did God really say, 'You must not eat from any tree in the garden'?" (Genesis 3:1). In fact, God did not say that at all. Satan was trying to sow confusion about what God had actually said. Eve's response, even though she corrected Satan, showed that she was uncertain about what God had said. Her phrase, "and you must not touch it," was her own invention.

Perhaps Eve was doing something that the rabbis of Jesus' day did intentionally. They added their own rules to God's laws, in an attempt to "build a hedge" around the law. If Eve could not touch the fruit, she certainly would not be able to eat it! Later Jesus would condemn this practice, for it led to nullifying "the word of God for the sake of your tradition" (Matthew 15:6).

"You Will Not Surely Die"

Satan's next step was to deny directly what God had said, and to offer an alternative. "God knows that when you eat of it your eyes will be opened, and you will be like God, knowing good and evil" (Genesis 3:4–5). In this, Satan was planting doubt about God's motives. God may have said X, but the truth is Y. God only said what He did to deprive you of something good.

How easily we fall into the trap of doubting God's motives! We fall short of being convinced that what God commands is for our benefit, not to deprive us of something good.

By this time Eve's confidence in and commitment to God was thoroughly undermined. She was unsure of what God had really said and no longer certain that God's warning was motivated by love for her rather than by selfish ambition of His own. So Genesis 3:6 tells us that Eve made her choice by relying on the appearance of the fruit (she saw that it was "good for food and pleasing to the eye") and on an uncertain but hoped-for result (it was "desirable for gaining wisdom"). How tragic! Appearances are hardly a basis for making good or godly decisions. The mere hope that our choices might possibly turn out well is no better. So Eve fell into the trap Satan set, and was deceived.

"Adam Was Not the One Deceived"

That statement, in 1 Timothy 2:14, alerts us to the true trap Satan set. Adam was not fooled by Satan's twisting of God's word. Adam knew very well that Satan was lying when Satan claimed, "You will not surely die," and promised that their eyes would be opened. What Adam's choice shows is that Adam, like Satan before him, yearned for independence.

Adam wanted to be his own god. Adam wanted to be the center of his universe, free to do what he wanted to do, when he wanted to do it.

This is the real test that each of us faces. Do we want to engage in spiritual warfare for the glory of God? Or do we want to take authority over evil spirits for our glory—because it makes us feel special, or makes us look special in the eyes of others?

This is also the issue that is presented in the temptations Satan posed when he approached a starving Jesus in the Judean wilderness. Jesus' responses to Satan's challenges are responses we will need to make, too, if we are to be God's warriors in the invisible war.

6

Jesus' First Temptation

Matthew and Luke present different orders in which the three temptations of Jesus took place. This is not an "error" in the Bible. It is simply that each author organizes his presentation to fit the theme of his book. Matthew presents Jesus as the Old Testament's promised king. The temptation he emphasizes, by placing it third, is Satan's promise to give Christ "all the kingdoms of the world and their splendor" (Matthew 4:8). Luke presents Jesus as the ideal human being. He emphasizes Satan's challenge to Him to leap from the pinnacle of the Temple, saying, "If you are the son of God," angels will catch "you . . . so that you will not strike your foot against a stone" (Luke 4:9–11). In these chapters we will follow Luke's order.

Both gospel records start with the same attempt by the tempter to sever Christ's allegiance to the Father. Luke says of the forty days Jesus was in the desert: "[Jesus] ate nothing during those days, and at the end of them he was hungry. The devil said to him, 'If you are the Son of God, tell this stone to become bread' " (Luke 4:2–3).

After a few days without food, a person is no longer hungry. But when the body's resources are used up, intense hunger hits. For most people this occurs around the thirtieth day of a fast. We can only imagine how great Christ's hunger must have been after forty days.

It was at this point of greatest weakness, when Jesus' physical resources must have been exhausted, that Satan chose to strike. And he struck at a truly vulnerable point, stating, "If you are the Son of God, tell this stone to become bread."

There are several grammatical constructions in Greek that are rendered *if* in English. In this case Satan used a construction that assumes the condition to be true. That is, Satan was not expressing doubt. He was saying, "Since You are the Son of God, act like it! Use Your powers to turn this stone into bread."

Neither Satan nor Jesus doubted that this was possible. Since Jesus was hungry, why not simply perform a minor miracle and feed Himself?

Christ responded by quoting a verse from the book of Deuteronomy: "It is written: 'Man does not live on bread alone' " (Luke 4:4). Matthew completes the quote: "but on every word that comes from the mouth of God" (Matthew 4:4; see Deuteronomy 8:3). The Deuteronomy context is striking. There Moses reminded the people of Israel that God had "led you all the way in the desert these forty years" (Deuteronomy 8:2). Now Christ was also in a desert, led there by God. And Satan was urging him to take matters into His own hands and act on His own initiative.

In Deuteronomy 8:2, Moses explained that God led the Israelites into the desert "to humble you and to test you in order to know what was in your heart, whether or not you would keep his commands." It was clear to Jesus that He was now facing this same test. He had been led by the Spirit into the desert and not provided with food. Would He, under the pressure of His hunger, "keep [God's] commands"?

Before we look more closely at Christ's response, we need to note one more thing. The first word Jesus uttered was *man. Man* does not live by bread alone. Yes, Satan was correct in saying *You are the Son of God.* But Jesus entered our world as a true human being. He would live a human life, experiencing all the pressures and the pain that we are heir to. Jesus would meet Satan's challenges not as the Son of God, but as an authentic human being. In this case, it was not Christ's weakness or His hunger that was the issue. The issue was simply this: Would Christ continue to depend upon the Holy Spirit to lead Him, or would He act on His own?

It was God's Spirit who led Jesus into the desert where He was being tempted by the devil. As a human being Jesus had no right to take matters into His own hands, to act apart from the Spirit's leading. Jesus' choices must not be driven by His situation or by His needs. Jesus must wait for a word from God, guiding Him down the path that God had chosen for His Son.

It is vitally important, as we approach spiritual warfare, that we adopt Jesus' attitude. We must be individuals who look to the Holy Spirit to lead us, and who respond to that leading. Only as we rely on the Spirit for both leading and power will we be ready to conduct spiritual warfare against the devil.

The writer of Hebrews looks back on Israel's wilderness years and draws an important lesson. He pictures the Israelites, drawn up at the borders of Canaan, hearing God's command to enter and conquer the land. But the Israelites were afraid, and hardened their hearts. The writer applies

45

the story, warning, "See to it, brothers, that none of you has a sinful, unbelieving heart that turns away from the living God" (Hebrews 3:12). Note that the writer identifies God as "living." Our God truly is the living God, a God who speaks to us in our todays. And so the writer says, "Today, if you hear his voice, do not harden your hearts" (Hebrews 3:7).

As the passage develops, we are reminded that God Himself is at rest (see Hebrews 4:11). This does not imply that God is inactive. He is totally involved in the flow of history and in our own lives, and certainly in the invisible war He is conducting against evil. God's rest implies that no situation can arise that God has not already planned for. Whatever men or demons may choose to do, God is ready with a response that will glorify Him, defeat Satan and lead us out of our wildernesses. As the writer says, "Everything is uncovered and laid bare before the eyes of him to whom we must give account" (Hebrews 4:13).

Jesus, facing a choice we will face time and time again, set us an example to follow. Satan will attempt to sidetrack us. He will goad us to rely on ourselves, to try to find our own way out of circumstances we find ourselves in. But Jesus, faced with this choice, responded that man does not live by bread alone. The true challenge we face is not how to solve our own problems. The true challenge is, Are we committed to listening for God's voice and, when He speaks to us, obeying?

And lest we think that God is not concerned with our circumstances and our needs, Matthew tells us that, after the devil left Jesus, "angels came and attended him" (Matthew 4:11).

7

Jesus' Second Temptation

Satan is persistent if nothing else. He and his demons will not stop trying to render God's people impotent and ineffective. He is intent on luring us away from the path God has for us.

We see one of his most effective strategies in the second temptation of Jesus.

> The devil led him up to a high place and showed him in an instant all the kingdoms of the world. And he said to him, "I will give you all their authority and splendor, for it has been given to me, and I can give it to anyone I want to. So if you worship me, it will all be yours."
>
> Luke 4:5–7

Actually, Satan was telling a half-truth. First John 5:19 tells us that "the whole world is under the control of the evil one." When used theologically, *world* (*kosmos*, Greek) refers to human society, the motives that drive it and the values that are expressed in its institutions. So, on the one hand, Satan offered Jesus the adulation of humanity, and, on the other, the satisfaction of every desire felt by a fallen humanity.

Adam had exchanged an intimate love relationship with his Creator for the prospect of independence. Satan offered Jesus what seemed to be a far greater prize. But the apostle John reminds us that "everything in the world—the cravings of sinful man, the lust of his eyes and the boasting of what he has and does—comes not from the Father but from the world" (1 John 2:16). A prize to be won by loving the world may seem desirable. But love for the world guarantees an empty, meaningless life, isolated from intimate relationship with God and void of the fulfillment that living in His will provides.

What Satan offered to Jesus, and what he offers to us when we set our hearts on the pleasures the world seems to provide, leads only to dissatisfaction and loss. And the price we pay is to worship one of Satan's fictions, whether money, fame or popularity.

It should be no surprise that Jesus once again returned to Deuteronomy and answered Satan with a quote from God's Word: "It is written: 'Worship the Lord your God and serve him only' " (Luke 4:8, quoting Deuteronomy 6:13). Nothing, and no one, is to take God's place as the focus of our desire.

Logos and Rhema

At this point I want to note that Jesus met every temptation with a word from Scripture. There are two terms in Greek translated "word" in our New Testament. One is *logos*, a general term for expression or communication. Jesus, as the "Word" (*logos*) of God, is the visible expression of the Creator, able to communicate who God is through His incarnation.

The other term translated "word" is *rhema*, which focuses our attention on a specific revelation of God's will. In responding to Satan, Jesus chose to quote a *rhema*, a specific word found in Scripture. Jesus, in remaining true to the Father, would take as His guide a specific *rhema*, and He would choose to live by it.

It is true that God has promised Christians the Holy Spirit. But it is also true that Scripture says the Holy Spirit will remind us of Jesus' teachings and bring them to our minds (see John 14:26). How vital then that we come to know God's Word as a familiar friend: Even the Holy Spirit cannot cause us to remember something we never learned! It was Jesus' familiarity with the older Testament that enabled the Spirit of God to bring to mind the specific *rhema* that guided Him in successfully resisting Satan's temptations.

Satan's Half-Truths

I noted that Satan was telling a half-truth. Satan does exercise authority over the world and can "give it to anyone" he wants. The problem with Satan's offer is that the devil is called a liar in Scripture, and the "father [source] of lies" (John 8:44). Satan's promises, however attractive they may seem, are never kept. All Satan offers is a fantasy that can never provide the fulfillment we seek.

But there is more to this temptation than meets the eye. Suppose Christ had been given authority over all the kingdoms of the world. How different human history would have been! Under Jesus there would have been no wars. Scripture pictures the Kingdom Jesus will rule as a kingdom of peace, where humans live long and satisfying lives. Imagine history without the world wars we have known in the past century, without the Holocaust, without the bloody carnage of terrorists' bombs.

In essence, Satan was tempting Jesus with the prospect of doing something good right now, without passing through the personal agony of the cross, and without having to witness the centuries of human suffering that have passed between then and now. But Jesus overcame the temptation to do something that must have seemed truly good. It was up to the Father to determine when and how God's Kingdom would come.

Think about it. Few of us have any a desire to worship and serve Satan. Yes, many are deceived into desiring worldly success and the accolades of the crowd. But the real temptation for us is the desire to do something we recognize as truly good.

In the 1960s Joseph Fletcher proposed what is called *situation ethics*. Noting Jesus' emphasis on loving God and one's neighbor, Fletcher argued that in making any decision all we need to do is to determine "the loving thing to do," and do it. If our understanding of the loving thing comes into conflict with a moral precept in Scripture, we are to choose the loving thing.

Fletcher's system breaks down at a number of points. Anyone who has ever heard of unintended consequences realizes that the outcomes of any choice are uncertain. Only God knows what choice is truly loving, and the guidelines He gives us in the Bible show us how to love God and to love others.

When Jesus was faced with a choice to do what must have seemed a loving and good thing, He trusted God's Word to guide Him. God had a plan, and although that plan called for Him to suffer, and for the final blessing of humanity to be delayed, Jesus would trust His Father.

As we undertake spiritual warfare, we, too, will be faced with choices, some of which seem to benefit others, but which violate guidelines laid down in God's Word. It is then we are to respond as Jesus did: "It is written, worship the Lord your God, and Him only shall you serve."

8

Jesus' Third Temptation

The third temptation Jesus faced was the most difficult of all. Christ had determined to meet Satan's challenges as an authentic human being, not in His character as God the Son. Satan's last challenge was directed against our most vulnerable point as human beings. Luke tells us,

> The devil led him to Jerusalem and had him stand on the highest point of the temple. "If you are the Son of God," he said, "throw yourself down from here. For it is written, 'He will command his angels concerning you to guard you carefully; they will lift you up in their hands, so that you will not strike your foot against a stone.'"
>
> Luke 4:9–11

The key to understanding this temptation is to know that Satan's *If* here is totally different from the *If* in the first temptation. Here the Greek construction tells us that Satan was saying, "If You are the Son of God—and I really don't believe You possibly could be—throw Yourself down."

It was a devastating challenge. The Spirit had led Jesus into a desert where He was alone and without food. Then Satan appeared to tempt Him. It must have seemed to Jesus that He had been abandoned by the Father.

So Satan sought to increase any doubts Jesus might have had. "If You are the Son of God—and surely God isn't treating You as a Son!—prove to Yourself that that's who You really are. After all, Scripture says that angels will catch the true Son of God so that not even His foot will strike a stone."

Again Jesus turned to Deuteronomy to respond. "It says: 'Do not put the Lord your God to the test' " (Luke 4:12; see Deuteronomy 6:16). Putting God to the test was what the Israelites had done after they were led into the wilderness by a fiery pillar of cloud. When the food and water ran out, they demanded a miracle, asking whether God was among them or not. Jesus' response to Satan showed a totally different attitude: I might be hurting. I might be under intense pressure. But I will trust God, not test Him.

There will be times when we feel isolated and alone, either completely inadequate to confront the evil spirits who are tormenting a person we are called to help, or worn out by their incessant voices of doubt or fear in our own lives and seemingly unable to break through. It is just such times when we feel we have been abandoned by God that we are most likely to beg for some sign of God's presence.

At such times we need to remember the meaning of the primary Old Testament name of God: *Yahweh*. That name occurs more than 2,500 times in the Old Testament, where it is rendered LORD in our English versions. The name was given to Moses just before he entered Egypt to free the Hebrew slaves, and is constructed on the Hebrew verb "to be." We might paraphrase its meaning as "The One Who Is Always Present."

What a significant name for the Hebrew slaves who saw God unleash His power to break Pharaoh's bonds and set them free! And God had told Moses, "This is my name forever, the name by which I am to be remembered from generation to generation" (Exodus 3:15). Israel was never to forget that, whatever the circumstances, God was present with them. The Exodus generation did forget. They tried to put God to the test, to make Him prove He was with them. But Jesus did not forget. Despite whatever doubts and fears He might have had as He met Satan's challenges in His humanity, Christ would put His trust in God as "The One Who Is Always Present."

This is perhaps the greatest challenge we face in engaging in spiritual warfare Jesus' way. In every situation we must walk by faith, confident that our God is present with us, and that Jesus is Lord.

Luke concludes his account of the temptation of Jesus by noting that "When the devil had finished all this tempting, he left him until an opportune time" (Luke 4:13).

Satan had failed to shake Jesus' reliance on the Father. He had failed to drive a wedge between them, as he had driven a wedge between Adam and the Creator. But Satan was not ready to give up. Satan left. But only until an opportune time.

As we engage in spiritual warfare, we need to remember that Satan will mount attack after attack. But, equipped with the Word of God and an unshakable confidence in God, we can have an important role in tearing down Satan's work.

Summary of Part 2

Personal Preparation

Believers are qualified to engage in spiritual warfare as adopted sons and daughters of God, who have been gifted with the Holy Spirit and given authority over evil spirits. But we need to be personally prepared to meet the challenges Satan will mount.

Adam and Eve failed the test of personal preparation by distorting God's Word, questioning God's motives and, ultimately, by choosing to live independent lives rather than commit to God's way.

Millennia later, Satan attempted to drive a similar wedge between Jesus and the Father. Satan failed to move Jesus to act independently of God in order to meet a physical need (the first temptation). Satan also failed to move Jesus to act in violation of God's will when he offered Him all the kingdoms of this world (the second temptation). And Satan failed to cause Jesus to doubt God when he pretended uncertainty about Jesus' identity as God's dearly loved Son (the third temptation).

Several things in these temptation reports are important for us as we seek to repel any attacks of demons or minister deliverance to those who are oppressed. First, Jesus chose to meet every temptation in His human rather than divine nature. Jesus used no resource that is not available to you and me. Second, Jesus' response to each temptation was to quote a *rhema*, a specific word of God that was relevant to the situation. He then committed Himself to obeying the Scripture quoted. Surely, if we are to be personally prepared for spiritual warfare, we must be students of God's Word.

What we learn from the temptation stories in Scripture is that to be personally prepared for spiritual warfare:

- We must know and understand God's Word;
- We must trust God's motives;
- We must not act independently of God's leading;
- We must be guided by God's Word rather than by our culture's ideas of what is "good";
- We must be confident that God is present, no matter how difficult our circumstances.

Part 3

The Context of Conquest

9

The Jesus Model

esus resisted the temptations Satan designed to undermine His relationship with the Father. In this, Jesus showed that He was personally fit to fulfill His mission.

Isaiah 42–53 depicts two "servants of the LORD." One is Israel, which fails to fulfill its mission to "display [God's] splendor" (Isaiah 49:3). The other is the Messiah, who will succeed as "a covenant for the people and a light for the Gentiles, to open eyes that are blind, to free captives from prison and to release from the dungeon those who sit in darkness" (Isaiah 42:6–7). Immediately after the temptations, Jesus set out on this mission. We see what happened in the stories that follow the temptation accounts.

Mark pictures Jesus teaching in a synagogue in Capernaum. But Christ's message was interrupted. "Just then a man in their synagogue who was possessed by an evil spirit cried out" (Mark 1:23). Jesus told the man to be quiet, and commanded the evil spirit, "Come out of him."

Luke tells the same story. First he explains that Jesus inaugurated His ministry in a synagogue in His hometown of Nazareth, where He read from the scroll of the prophet Isaiah and announced its fulfillment (see Luke 4:14–21). Luke then relays that Jesus "went down to Capernaum," and on the Sabbath began to teach in the synagogue there (verse 31). But He was interrupted by "a man possessed by a demon, an evil spirit" (verse 33). " 'Be quiet,' Jesus said sternly. 'Come out of him!' Then the demon threw the man down before them all and came out without injuring him" (verse 35).

Matthew's account is in complete harmony with these two accounts. Matthew states that Jesus left Nazareth and went to live in Capernaum, to fulfill another of Isaiah's prophecies about light dawning in that land (see Matthew 4:13–17). Matthew does not tell the specific story of the event in the Capernaum synagogue, but he does tell us that after Jesus called His twelve disciples, He began immediately to go "throughout Galilee, teaching in their synagogues, preaching the good news of the kingdom, and healing every disease and sickness" (verse 23). The result was that news about Him "spread all over." Those suffering with various diseases, including "the demon-possessed," were brought to Jesus for healing (verse 24).

I doubt that the neighbors of the man who spoke up in that synagogue in Capernaum had any idea an evil spirit was present in his life. He was probably, to all appearances, a good, religiously observant Jew, a neighbor everyone knew. But the demon was so disturbed by the presence of Jesus, whom he recognized as "the Holy One of God" (Mark 1:24), that he could not help revealing his presence.

In other cases family, friends and neighbors did recognize demonic influence and brought the individuals to Jesus. Please note that *in neither of these situations did Jesus set out to hunt demons.* Instead, as Jesus taught and preached, demons were exposed.

Let me state this again: In these accounts Jesus did not go looking for demons. Jesus ran into demons while preaching and teaching. The demons were revealed in the context of His ministry.

Questions Close to Home

The other day a young man I will call "Kyle" wrote me by email and then phoned. Kyle had met two men through his work at a YMCA and befriended them. As he got to know them better, he realized that both seemed in the grip of some evil that had a firm hold on their lives. As Kyle spent time with them, he learned that both felt the evil, but they did not know what it was or what to do about it. Because Kyle is the kind of person who cares about others, he became more and more troubled. What could he do to free these men from the evil spirits that seemed to bind them?

In this, Kyle was walking down the path Jesus had taken. As Kyle ministered to his two friends, prayed for them and encouraged them to come to church, a spirit of evil was revealed in each individual.

It happened that a man who had been Kyle's employer had attended one of my Freedom Workshops and suggested Kyle contact me. So Kyle wrote to me and then phoned, because he has compassion for each of these men and a deep desire to conquer the evil spirits that torment them. Kyle simply yearns to set them free.

Kyle did not set out to hunt demons. It was only through ministry to men who had become friends, and discovering how oppressed they were, that he began to ask how to conquer evil spirits.

Finding Answers

It is fascinating that in every case where Jesus confronted an evil spirit, He cast the demon out immediately. Again, Jesus did not go in search of demons (we will talk about this more in chapter 11). But whenever in the context of His ministry a demon did show, Jesus dealt with it decisively. This is what impressed me so much about Kyle. He became aware of the possible demonization of two men he was seeking to reach for Christ. As Kyle sensed the struggles they were having, and felt the evil that oppressed them, he was filled with compassion. What Kyle wants to do now is learn how to deal with the demons that trouble his friends. And, in addition, Kyle feels a deepening desire to minister to others who are also oppressed by evil spirits.

I met with Kyle yesterday morning at a bakery about halfway between his home and mine. He asked me, "What do I do?"

On the one hand, the answer is, "In the name of Jesus, command the spirits to leave." In fact, this is *the* answer. But, of course, there is more involved, more that we want to understand.

The chances are that if you are actively ministering to other people, you will need to know what I told Kyle, and much more. I often receive email telling of an adult child or other relative or friend whom the writer suspects might be demonized. Perhaps you are concerned about one of your loved ones or a person you have been ministering to. You might have wondered, How can I tell if demons have a grip on a person's life? Or, How would I go about delivering that person if demonization is involved?

Or, in the more general sense, How do I know if demons are behind some of the struggles my friends and I are facing?

How do I know if a demon is trying to influence my thoughts or actions?

We have looked at the source of the invisible war that is going on all around us, and we have looked at personal preparation for spiritual warfare. There are just a couple of more things to consider before we answer the "how" questions.

10

Deliverance Ministry Ground Rules

One of the most significant things that Jesus did is recorded in Luke 6:12: "When morning came, he called his disciples to him and chose twelve of them." Frequently the word *disciple* is used in the gospels simply to indicate a follower of Jesus. But it is used in a special sense when applied to the twelve men listed in the Luke passage, who are also called the "apostles" (meaning ones sent on a mission to represent another's interests). In first-century Judaism, becoming the "disciple" of a particular teacher or rabbi meant taking on a special role and responsibilities. Discipleship was the only path a person could take to become a rabbi himself. It was the one and only way a Jewish man was trained for spiritual or religious leadership.

This was one of the things that confounded the Jewish leaders who were Jesus' opponents. Christ had never been a disciple of a rabbi or teacher of the Law. No wonder they were "amazed and asked, 'How did this man get such learning without having studied?'" (John 7:15).

While Jesus had not followed the only recognized path, it was clear the twelve ordinary men Jesus chose would need to become His disciples in the traditional sense. A disciple abandoned his old life to spend all his time with his teacher. The disciple was expected to observe his teacher's way of life and listen intently to his teachings. While the rabbi was responsible for meeting the basic financial needs of his disciples, the disciples were expected to serve him and to do all they could to free the rabbi for his own ministry. Thus, when the gospels speak of the Twelve as Jesus' disciples, they view them as men whom Jesus was training to become future leaders of whatever movement He intended to establish.

It was a costly thing to become a disciple. We see this expressed by Peter when he said, "We have left everything to follow you!" (Matthew 19:27). Peter was right. He and the others had left their homes, their businesses, their families, their very identities to become disciples of Jesus. Luke 6:40 describes the expected result. Jesus said, "A student [a disciple, a learner] is not above his teacher, but everyone who is fully trained will be like his teacher." The disciples were on track, not just to learn from Jesus, but to be transformed toward Christ's likeness. And to participate in His mission.

Three Ground Rules

There are many important ideas in these texts. Here are three points for us to observe, particularly if we intend to minister to someone who is under demonic attack of any sort, or where demonic influence is seen in our homes or even our pets.

First, we need in our training some element of discipleship. Jesus trained some of His followers to serve as future leaders;

this is something that Christians have tried to do from the beginning. But in our day, too great an emphasis is placed on mastery of information rather than personal transformation. Yes, a disciple needs to know God's truth. But we all need to experience personal growth that cannot be taught in seminary classrooms. Scripture reminds us that we are called to disciple each other as we share our lives with other believers. As we meet, often in small groups, sometimes with just a committed Christian friend, to share our lives and what Jesus is teaching us, we "become mature" and grow toward "attaining to the whole measure of the fullness of Christ" (Ephesians 4:13). Today we followers of Jesus are called to disciple one another.

Second, we need to note that the ministry of casting out evil spirits is not reserved for ordained leaders. Luke 10:1 tells us that "the Lord appointed seventy-two others and sent them." That word *others* is especially significant. The 72 were followers of Jesus and committed to Him, but they were not in training to become leaders! They were ordinary believers, nameless here and unrecognized in the biblical text.

Still, these ordinary believers were Jesus' representatives. And while on their mission, they discovered that even they could cast out demons in Jesus' name (see Luke 10:17)! We need to recognize the importance of affirming the gifts of the laity, including the fact that any lay person as well as any ordained person can minister freedom to the oppressed by driving out evil spirits.

Third, we need to emphasize team ministry, not individual ministry. We need to remember that Jesus never sent His followers on a mission alone. After many months spent with Jesus, perhaps even years, Jesus "called his twelve disciples to him and gave them authority to drive out evil spirits and to heal every disease and sickness" (Matthew 10:1). The parallel passages in Mark and Luke make it clear that Jesus' twelve disciples were not sent out alone. As Mark 6:7 informs us, "He sent them out two by two."

When Jesus sent out the 72 "others," Luke 10:1 makes sure that we know these also were sent out "two by two ahead of him to every town and place where he was about to go." I suspect there are a number of reasons for Jesus' two-by-two strategy. One, certainly, is that when we emphasize individuals, we steal glory from Jesus and exalt a human being inappropriately. Another is that—particularly as we seek to help those who are oppressed by demonization—we need prayer support from someone sharing in that ministry. It did not matter which of the two disciples, or which of the two "others," took the lead. Theirs was a shared ministry, a team ministry.

Building on That Foundation

Once we understand the ground rules for ministering to the demonically oppressed, we can move into active training. In Jesus' relationships with the Twelve and the "others," we see a pattern that we can follow today.

Step One: Observe

Jesus took the lead in teaching and in driving out demons. At first it was the disciples' role simply to observe. Jesus did the work; the Twelve and the "others" watched. As they watched, not only did they see what Jesus did but their confidence in Christ's ability to master evil spirits grew.

Step Two: Practice under Supervision

Next, Jesus' followers took the initiative. They exercised the authority Jesus gave them and drove out evil spirits themselves. At this stage none of these followers was expected to act on his own. They ministered by twos, as teams. Also note that when the Twelve and the 72 were sent out, Jesus gave them careful directions (see Matthew 10:5–42; Luke 10:2–16). And when a particular mission was accomplished, they debriefed, reporting to Jesus and being further instructed by Him (see Luke 10:17–24).

Step Three: Train Others

Finally, those in spiritual training entered ministry themselves. This is illustrated in Acts 10. Peter, now in the role of teacher and, thus, ministering without another of the disciples, brought along "some of the brothers from Joppa" (verse 23) so they could observe him and learn from him as he ministered.

This simple, three-step pattern is something that is adaptable to any time or place, and vital in deliverance ministry. First, watch and learn. In time, working in teams, confront the evil spirits while the discipler guides and debriefs. In the end, those who have been so trained will continue to minister deliverance, now with teams of their own that they can equip for this essential ministry.

11

The Role of Friends

Sometimes the little words in Scripture, words we tend to pass over because they seem unimportant, express powerful truths. Take, for instance, Matthew 9:32: "While they were going out, a man who was demon-possessed [demonized] and could not talk was brought to Jesus."

Looking at this verse we tend to fasten on certain elements of Matthew's description. We see a human being who was being oppressed by a demon. And this particular demon made the man mute and unable to speak. There was only one person who could help, and that was Jesus. As the story continues we see that Jesus drove out the spirit, and afterward the man spoke.

It is likely, if we were to teach or to preach a sermon on this text, that we would emphasize the power of Jesus to transform the demonized man's experience. With the demon driven out, the mute man was completely restored, and for the first time in however long, he could speak. No wonder "the crowd was amazed" (Matthew 9:33).

But there is one word in this sentence that is easy to overlook, yet it conveys an important message. That word is *brought*. This man did not seek Jesus out. Unlike the leper in Mark 1:40, the demonized man did not come to Jesus and beg Him on his knees, "If You are willing, You can make me clean." No, the mute man in Matthew 9:32 had to be "brought" to Jesus.

This raises an important question: How many demonized persons whose stories are included in the gospels came to Jesus on their own, asking His help? The answer is none!

Yes, people often brought their sick friends to Jesus to be healed, just as they brought the demonized. But many sick persons searched Jesus out on their own accord. Yet there is no record of any demonized individual seeking Jesus out so that the demon oppressing him might be expelled.

We do see situations in which Jesus was ministering and demonized individuals appeared in the crowd. Mark 3:7–11 describes a time when great masses of people were crowding around Jesus—so many that Christ had to teach from a small fishing boat. In that swirling, pushing mass were some who were demonized, just as there had been a demonized man in the synagogue at Capernaum. Mark tells us that "whenever the evil spirits saw him, they fell down before him and cried out, 'You are the Son of God' " (verse 11).

This acknowledgment of Jesus' identity was hardly a plea for help. It was a confession forced from unwilling beings by the glory the demons could see despite its masking by human flesh. Not one of those demonized persons on that or any other occasion came to Jesus for deliverance on his or her own. In each case of driving out demons reported in the gospels, the demonized person was either among the crowds when Jesus was ministering, or the demonized person was brought to Jesus by friends or relatives.

But What about Legion?

As we make discoveries in Scripture, we have to be careful to look at all the evidence. The story of the man demonized by Legion (see Mark 5:1–20), for instance, would seem to contradict my point.

Mark tells us what happened when Jesus and His disciples traveled across Lake Galilee to a district that was more Gentile than Jewish. "When Jesus got out of the boat, a man with an evil spirit came from the tombs to meet him" (Mark 5:2). At first glance, this verse would seem to contradict my point about all the demonized being brought to Jesus. But when we look at the verse more closely, we find something interesting.

First, the word *came* is supplied by the translators. The Greek text simply states that a man with an evil spirit, from the tombs, met Jesus. Even more importantly, the word translated "meet" (*hypanteo*) is an unusual word. It is most often translated "met," twice "went out to meet" and once "oppose" as "to meet in battle." The point is that this verb does not tell us the purpose for which an individual goes out to meet someone.

So the question is, What do the accounts of Jesus' meeting with Legion tell us about how to understand this word and translate the verse? The context question is answered in Matthew 8:28, which describes the demonized man as "so violent that no one could pass that way." What we see is a strong, hostile, demonized individual who attacked anyone who came near. And that is what he was doing—coming out to attack the people who had just landed onshore. But when he recognized Jesus, he reacted as all other demonized persons

71

did: The man fell on his knees, and the demon acknowledged Jesus as the Son of God. And in terror, the demon begged, "Swear to God that you won't torture me!" (Mark 5:7).

How then should we understand Mark 5:2? I believe it is more accurate to translate it this way: "When Jesus got out of the boat, a man with an evil spirit rushed out to oppose Him" or, even better, "rushed out to harm Him." Imagine the demon's shock when he realized that he was encountering Jesus and was compelled to kneel and submit to Him.

So we are on solid ground when we observe that little word *brought*. As far as the gospel accounts are concerned, the sick could come to Jesus on their own. But the demonized were either caught unexpectedly in a synagogue or in a crowd where Jesus was teaching, or were brought to Jesus by someone else.

Please note: While it is important for us to be aware of possible demonization in a friend or loved one, we also need to be cautious. Sometimes the symptoms we see are evidence of a naturally caused illness or a psychological problem caused by some traumatic experience. In such cases, introducing the idea of demonization can be harmful. It is wise first to check out possible organic causes with medical doctors, and possible traumatic causes with a trained therapist. Most important, we need to seek guidance from the Holy Spirit as to what is going on in our friend's or loved one's life.

Friends and Family

I have known cases where individuals who have come for counseling have been surprised to discover that at least part of their problem was caused by evil spirits. I have also known individuals who were profoundly demonized, yet were drawn to the Freedom Workshops I conduct on the armor of God (see *The Full Armor of God*, Chosen, 2013). I would not argue that it is impossible for even a profoundly demonized individual to take the initiative and look for someone to drive out the demons. I would argue, however, that the demon would do everything he could to prevent his host from seeking effective help.

Most important, I believe we see an important pattern in the gospels. Demonized individuals need to be brought to someone who can help. It is the responsibility of friends and family who suspect or who sense a person is demonized to get that individual the help he or she needs to break free.

If you do not yet feel that you can help in that situation, you might look for someone in the Christian community around you—your own church or another church—who has experience in driving out evil spirits. If you cannot locate such a person, you might contact the International Society of Deliverance Ministers to see if any of their members live in your area. You can search the Internet to find the contact information for ISDM.

But be willing, as the Holy Spirit leads you, simply to follow the process outlined in the pages of this book and cast out any evil spirits yourself. If you do choose to do this, please follow the guidelines given here to protect yourself and the individual—particularly enlisting the support of others who will pray as you and your co-minister deal with the demon(s).

You can certainly be victorious as you engage in spiritual warfare Jesus' way.

Summary of Part 3

The Context of Conquest

Jesus kept His focus on the ministry to which He was called. In the context of that ministry, He met demonized individuals and drove out the demons. As Jesus' reputation grew, people brought other demonized individuals to Him to be freed. We, also, are to focus on the ministry to which God calls us, whether it is a public ministry like teaching or a personal ministry to individuals we meet through our employment or our neighborhood or a church group. As we become aware of others who seem to be oppressed, we can learn from Jesus how to conquer the evil spirits that trouble them.

As we follow Christ's ministry, we note that He equipped His followers as well as gave them authority to drive out demons. One of the important features of Christ's equipping was to emphasize team ministry. Both the twelve disciples and the 72 "others" Jesus sent out to preach and to cast out demons were sent out by twos. Even as we move into Acts and the epistles, we see an emphasis on team ministry, although at times an apostle like Peter would carry out ministry as sole leader, while bringing along a support team (see Acts 10:23).

But the gospels also suggest that there is another role that is significant in deliverance ministry. Not one of the persons whom Jesus delivered from demonic presences took the initiative and came to Jesus looking for release. In each case recorded in the gospels, friends or family "brought" the demonized person to Jesus. How important, then, to be in a Christian community where the reality of demonization is recognized, and possible symptoms of demonization are understood!

Part 4

Defining Demonization

12

The Reliable Source

Throughout history, humans have believed that a hidden, invisible world inhabited by spirits exists. For most of history these spirits—gods, goddesses, ghosts, nature spirits, angels and demons—have been regarded with suspicion. The gods and goddesses of the ancient world were capricious, not to be trusted. They might shower favor on a hero one moment and then doom him to some horrible fate the next. It is no wonder that supernatural beings like demons were feared by most people.

Appealing to what people have believed "throughout history," of course, is hardly the way to determine what is true. For centuries people in the West believed the earth was flat, as well as believing that the sun rotated around our tiny planet. How then can we get reliable information about demons and the spirit world? Here are some sources that people have relied on—and still rely on—for their beliefs about demons.

- Social consensus—things that "everybody believes"
- Tradition—practices handed down from generation to generation
- The dictates of accepted authority figures
- Reports of others' experiences
- Personal experiences
- Revelation

The things that "everybody believes" generally have deep roots in a culture. If we were to go to any of several Third World nations we would find that nearly everyone believes that sickness or misfortune is caused by the spirits of dead ancestors who are angry because they have not been appropriately honored by the living. While nearly everyone in such cultures shares this belief, we can hardly consider this to be a reliable source of information.

Tradition formulates responses to whatever it is that "everyone believes." In the cultures mentioned above, tradition requires rituals honoring the dead and offering them food or gifts. Again, tradition is hardly a source of reliable information, or a guide to responding to the supernatural.

The dictates of accepted authority figures definitely color our beliefs. In the Middle Ages the Church was the accepted authority, and shaped the culture's view of angels and demons. In modern times, science has become the accepted authority—and the basis for denial of the existence of the supernatural. Still, a 2011 television network (CBS) poll indicated that eight in ten Americans believed in angels, while a Baylor University poll in 2007 showed that 45.8 percent of Americans affirmed a belief in the existence of demons. It is fair to say, however, that these beliefs do not shape the way Americans live. Instead, we act as though the material world is the only real world. Belief in angels or demons has little impact on most people's lives and is no help in understanding the nature or the activity of demons.

Beliefs about demons are also shaped by the reported experiences of others. Books and movies about evil spirits invading a person's home, images of violent exorcisms and claims about the paranormal all shape the beliefs within society. While many of these stories are reputedly "based on" someone's experiences, the details and the interpretations of what supposedly happened tend to be exaggerated. Again, these can hardly be viewed as reliable sources. On the other hand, books by reputable authors like C. Fred Dickenson, Ed Murphy, Charles Kraft and many others are a rich source of information about demonization and how a Christian can confront and conquer evil spirits.

Another source of information is personal experience. The early Church fathers reported that casting out demons was a common phenomenon, and many books describe the experiences of casting out demons today. I have also communicated with individuals who claim to be or to have been demonized. I have no reason to challenge the reality of the experiences shared. But how a person interprets his or her experience may or may not be reliable.

There is, however, one source of information about demons and demonization that is totally reliable. That source is revelation, recorded for us in the Scriptures. Not only is God's Word a trustworthy source of information about demons and demonization, it also enables us to evaluate beliefs gleaned from other sources. In particular, Scripture provides a template to lay over experiences with the supernatural in order to gauge authenticity.

That is why this book focuses on reports in the four gospels of Jesus' teaching on and His confrontations with demons. If we are to define and understand demonization, we need to start here and use the insights gained in order to understand the experiences others report.

Thus, we begin our exploration by determining how the gospels depict what is called in the original Greek *daimonizomai*—demonization.

Putting Demons into Perspective

In the first section of this book, we looked at the Bible's depiction of an invisible war taking place "in the heavenlies," a New Testament term for the spiritual universe that lies alongside or above our own material universe. We saw that this spiritual universe was created before the material universe, and it was originally the home of God and of the angels He created. We saw that one of these angels led a rebellion against God in an attempt to supplant the Creator, and that he was followed by a great number of angels. The leader of the rebellion became Satan, and the angels that followed him became the beings the Bible identifies as demons or evil spirits.

The early chapters of Genesis and the book of Job reveal several important things about the abilities of the evil spirits ranged against God. Satan was able to speak through an agent to Adam and Eve in his successful attempt to alienate human beings from the Lord. Satan is also capable of causing events in the material universe. Evil spirits arranged raids on Job's herds, killing the herdsmen (see Job 1:14–15, 17), caused fire that destroyed Job's flocks and shepherds (see 1:16), and stirred up a windstorm that caused the death of Job's children (see 1:18–19). It is clear from these extreme examples that evil spirits have the ability to affect the circumstances of our lives. But this kind of demonic activity is never identified in Scripture as "demonization."

Nor does the Bible emphasize the role of evil spirits in shaping our circumstances. There are a few references, of course, to Satan's "outside" activities. The apostle Paul notes that despite multiple efforts to visit the Thessalonians he could not, because "Satan stopped us" (1 Thessalonians 2:18). Paul does not explain how Satan blocked his attempts to visit this young church, but manipulation of Paul's circumstances is clearly implied.

We should take seriously the concept that an invisible war is going on around us at all times, and that we might be targets. When we command evil spirits not to hinder our arrival time for a meeting, or ask God to provide angels to superintend the processing of important papers, we are simply taking seriously the potential impact of the spiritual realm on our daily lives. Unlike most of the 45.8 percent of Americans who report that they believe in demons, we actually take demonic activity seriously and use the resources God provides to protect ourselves from them.

While the Bible does address what evil spirits do "outside" us, Scripture is particularly concerned with what they can do within us—and that is the focus of the chapters in this part. We will see this as we explore the gospel accounts of Jesus' confrontations with demons. It is here, in the gospels, that the word *daimonizomai* appears often. Unfortunately, this Greek term has been translated into English as "demon-possessed," even though the word *possessed* is never found in the original text. What is found is the single Greek word that refers to a condition we should simply call "demonization."

Insights into Demonization

As we look at the uses of this term in the gospels, we are struck by several repeated elements, which are illustrated in a text we viewed earlier:

> In the synagogue there was a man possessed by a demon, an evil spirit. He cried out at the top of his voice, "Ha! What do you want with us, Jesus of Nazareth? Have you come to destroy us? I know who you are—the Holy One of God!"
>
> "Be quiet!" Jesus said sternly. "Come out of him!" Then the demon threw the man down before them all and came out without injuring him.
>
> Luke 4:33–35

First, it is clear that the terms *demon* and *evil spirit* refer to the same kind of being. It is also clear—from the fact that the demon spoke to Jesus, stated that he "knew" certain things, asked a question about what Christ intended to do to the group of which he was a member and used the personal pronoun *I*—that demons are personal beings, not simply "influences." In the same sense that we humans are persons, with the ability to think, to understand, to feel and to make choices, so demons are persons, as well.

Second, it is clear that demons (evil spirits) are the active enemies of God and His Holy One. They are, by definition, "evil" (in this text the Greek word is *akatharsia*, "unclean," a term indicating that the evil spirits are morally corrupt).

Third, the presence of the demonized man in a synagogue reminds us that nearly all those described as demonized in the gospels were members of the Old Testament's covenant community. That is, nearly everyone who is described as demonized must be assumed to be a believer unless there is specific evidence to the contrary. This suggests that demons *target* believers! It is God's people rather than the devil's children (see John 8:44) that demons attack.

Fourth, it is also clear from the fact that Jesus told the demon to "come out of him," and that the text adds that the demon "came out without injuring him," that in some sense the demon was "inside" the demonized man.

Finally, it is also clear that the beings that demonize believers are subject to Jesus and are unable to resist Him.

A Definition of *Demonization*

At this point it is possible to come up with a working definition of *demonization*. We might refine this definition later, but we need to be clear about what demonization basically is. Taking this Luke text as representative of what we find in other gospel passages, we can say that:

> *Demonization* is "the presence of an evil personality (a demon) *within* an individual."

This does not mean or imply that a demonized person is controlled by an evil presence. He or she typically might not even be aware of the demon or demons. It says simply that from a position *within* the human personality the demon has a unique opportunity to influence an individual's thoughts, emotions and choices. This is different from the sporadic attacks of demons on an individual from the *outside*—attacks that need to be repelled, but that can generally be dispatched without great effort once they are recognized.

Just what *demonization* means for the individual is something we will explore in this part. And, while we can make no definitive statement about the personal relationships that the individuals who are described as "demonized" in the gospels had with God, it is likely that the majority of the demonized were believers. At least one, a woman Jesus described as a "daughter of Abraham" (Luke 13:16), certainly was.

It is uncomfortable for some to think that believers are vulnerable to demonization. But we could hardly expect Satan and his evil angels to leave us alone. After all, we followers of Jesus are their primary enemies! Why should they focus their efforts on those who pose no threat to Satan's dark kingdom?

The encouraging thing to remember is that the Christ who commanded "Come out of him!" is Lord. In His name we can and do conquer evil spirits.

13

Symptoms of Demonization

Is it demons?"

That is a question I hear often.

How can I tell if that temptation I struggle to overcome is energized by demons?

How can I tell if a chronic illness doctors just can't seem to help is being driven by demons?

How can I tell if my adolescent, whose whole character seems to have changed and who has even threatened to kill us, is demonized?

How can I tell if the voice I seem to hear speaking inside me is the Holy Spirit or one of Satan's evil spirits?

Are there specific symptoms or markers that can help us determine the presence of demons within an individual? When we read books written by those experienced in casting out demons, we are likely to find lists of characteristics the authors say are indicators.

Generally, in the case of demonization, these lists lean toward the more extreme or severe indicators—such as cursing God and man, rage or physical violence and even doubt that one is saved. I have encountered these strong indicators, as have most deliverance ministers.

And, in fact, the gospels are filled with reports of Jesus casting demons out of individuals who were significantly disabled. In many cases a disability, whether blindness or crippled legs, had a natural cause. In such cases Jesus simply healed the suffering individual, even giving sight to a man born blind (see John 9:1–7). But in other cases the physical disability *was* triggered by evil spirits, and healing required that Jesus cast the evil spirit out.

A prime example of this kind of demonic activity was in a woman described in Luke 13, who was "bent over and could not straighten up at all." The text explicitly states that she "had been crippled by a spirit for eighteen years" (Luke 13:11) until Jesus set her free.

But more often than not, in Jesus' day and ours, the evidence is less striking. Think again of the demonized man in Luke 4, who sat quietly among the worshipers in the synagogue until Jesus began to speak, and we are reminded that demons can be active even when there are no obvious symptoms otherwise.

As far as the gospels are concerned, then, we have one case in a synagogue where it seems no external symptoms marked the man as demonized, and another case where a persistent, crippling disability indicated a woman's demonization. We need to make sure we do not test for demons only when the symptoms *are* obvious.

So what symptoms might alert us to the presence of demons? The story of Legion, which we discussed in chapter 11, noting that this man rushed toward Jesus with the intent of causing Him harm, is one that provides much insight into symptoms of demonization. The story is told by Matthew, Mark and, in the following passage, by Luke.

When Jesus stepped ashore, he was met by a demon-possessed man from the town. For a long time this man had not worn clothes or lived in a house, but had lived in the tombs. When he saw Jesus, he cried out and fell at his feet, shouting at the top of his voice, "What do you want with me, Jesus, Son of the Most High God? I beg you, don't torture me!" For Jesus had commanded the evil spirit to come out of the man. Many times it had seized him, and though he was chained hand and foot and kept under guard, he had broken his chains and had been driven by the demon into solitary places.

Luke 8:27–29

In a parallel account in Matthew, where two men are mentioned, the text tells us that the demoniacs "were so violent than no one could pass that way" (Matthew 8:28).

Mark adds two important details. Mark tells us that "night and day among the tombs and in the hills he would cry out and cut himself with stones" (Mark 5:5). And Mark notes that when Jesus got out of the boat, "a man with an evil spirit came from the tombs to meet him" (5:2), and even more graphically states that "when he saw Jesus from a distance, he ran and fell on his knees in front of him" (5:6).

Luke sums up the result of Jesus' casting out the many demons that infested this demonized man. When the people of the neighborhood came out to see what had happened, "they found the man from whom the demons had gone out, sitting at Jesus' feet, dressed and in his right mind" (Luke 8:35).

Most incidents of demonization reported in the gospels focus on the demons' operating through physical disabilities. Yet in the gospel reports of the man inhabited

87

by Legion, we see a wide range of symptoms that could possibly point to demonization. These symptoms fall into different categories.

Social Symptoms of Demonization

Luke tells us that the demoniac was "from the town." Social relations in the first century were extremely important. A person's identity was rooted in how his community perceived him, and that community was vitally important to his well-being. Yet this man left his family and his community to live "in the tombs." In first-century Judaism, anyone who touched a dead body or even a tomb became ritually unclean, and was isolated from the community until he had undergone cleansing. It is clear that the demoniac was isolating himself from other people. It is also clear from the effort to bind him with chains that the community had not given up on him. They were struggling to draw him back into normality.

One of the most important symptoms of possible demonization today is a person's intentional efforts to isolate himself from his family and friends. He or she might stop seeing friends, might spend less and less time with loved ones, more and more time alone. Efforts to reach out and draw him or her back into closer relationship will tend to be rejected. It is significant that in recent mass murders the killer is typically described as a "loner."

Interpersonal Symptoms of Demonization

Matthew describes the man as "so violent that no one could pass that way" (Matthew 8:28). The demoniac was actively aggressive, hostile and violent. It was dangerous for anyone to come near him, for he was bent on attacking anyone in his vicinity.

Most of those who come to me with concerns about loved ones are most upset about change they see from a once loving and responsive individual into one who is increasingly bitter and hostile. Typically the attacks described are verbal; bitter, hateful words are spoken that gradually give way to threats. But hostility can quickly morph into violence. One of my best friends, who has dealt often with the demonized, says that he has never dealt with a physically abusive spouse where demonization was not involved.

Combined with a drift toward isolation, increasingly hostile behavior laden with threats of violence is one of the clearest symptoms of possible demonization. Such threats must be taken seriously.

Moral Symptoms of Demonization

The description in Luke tells us that this demonized man "for a long time" had "not worn clothes or lived in a house" (Luke 8:27). In first-century Judaism, the moral code emphasized modesty. One of the great scandals of the time was that foreign gladiators, imported for games held by the Romans, thought nothing of walking through the streets of Jerusalem wearing nothing but their hats! The depiction of this man as without clothing is especially significant for that culture. It suggests an individual who has abandoned moral restraints and has adopted what is essentially a non-moral, if not immoral, attitude.

By abandoning moral restraints I am not thinking primarily of sexual sin, although this may be involved. Morality at heart involves respecting other persons and valuing them enough to consider their well-being. When an individual loses concern for others, that person has abandoned morality and the moral code. The choice of the demoniac to go naked is extremely significant given the values of his community—as is any action by a person today that shows he or she no longer takes the feelings and values of others into consideration.

Mental Symptoms of Demonization

Luke commented that after Jesus expelled the demons, the demoniac was "sitting at Jesus' feet, dressed and in his right mind" (Luke 8:35). This is doubly significant. He was now dressed, morally reoriented to his community. And he was "in his right mind." Under the influence of the demons the man had been "out of his mind."

The word translated "right mind" here is a compound constructed on the root *phroneo*. The underlying idea expressed is that of thinking or judging clearly and correctly. A demonized person's thought processes might be distorted, and his capacity to evaluate events and situations, or even his own plans, might be corrupted. So another symptom of possible demonization is that a person says and thinks things that seem "crazy"—distorted and foundationless.

Physical Symptoms of Demonization

Most accounts of evil spirits in the gospels feature some physical symptom of the demon's presence, such as an illness or serious physical disability or unusual physical expression. When Jesus cast out the demons, the individual was freed from the physical disability, as well.

In the case of the demoniac in Luke 8, the physical symptom was an amazing burst of strength, which enabled the demonized man to break chains used to bind him. While demons are likely involved in cases of persistent chronic illnesses that do not respond to medical treatment, we should not expect physical symptoms to be the primary marker of demonic oppression. Nor should we expect every physical problem to disappear when a demon is exorcised.

Psychological Symptoms of Demonization

Mark provides a detail not found in the other gospels. He tells us that "night and day among the tombs and in the hills he [the demoniac] would cry out and cut himself with stones" (Mark 5:5). While much contemporary research explores the roots of self-mutilation (cutting) by young women, the act itself seems to be an expression of self-loathing and evidence of overwhelming anxiety or despair. Whatever their roots in an individual's experience, shame and guilt seem to be present, often resulting in self-hatred as well as a deep sense of personal inadequacy.

While demons do not cause such psychological symptoms, demons do enhance and exaggerate emotions that are already present, stripping away any sense of self-worth and value.

Spiritual Symptoms of Demonization

Writers on deliverance often stress a demonized person's antagonism to the things of God, such as Scripture, Christian music and church. But Mark's account raises questions. Mark tells us that the man with the evil spirit "came from the tombs to meet" Jesus (Mark 5:2). We saw earlier that the initial motive of the man probably was to attack and drive away Jesus' party. Later Mark adds that "when he saw Jesus from a distance, he ran and fell on his knees in front of him. He shouted at the top of his voice, 'What do you want with me, Jesus, Son of the Most High God?' " (verses 6–7). Once Jesus was recognized, the man came closer, even though the demons in him were terrified.

Whatever the motives of the demons in approaching Jesus, the demons did not totally control the man they victimized. While the demons were repelled by Christ, the man experienced an attraction to Jesus at the same time.

Spiritual ambivalence is often present when a believer is demonized. The Christian wants to pray, but evil thoughts intrude. He goes to church but cannot stay awake during the sermon. He tries to read the Bible but cannot seem to grasp the meaning of the words. This pattern of ambivalence toward spiritual things seems far more characteristic of demonization than constant, open hostility.

As we look through these symptoms that point to possible demonization, it should be clear that each symptom can have causes other than evil spirits. It does not require demons to make a person hostile or violent. Physical disabilities can have natural causes, with no demonic involvement at all. Many have abandoned moral restraints on their own initiative, without the urging of evil spirits. We can even experience ambiguity in our relationships with the Lord, as anyone who too often promises to have a devotional time "tomorrow—when things aren't so hectic" should recognize.

Even though the symptoms described here do not provide definitive proof of demonization, it is important to understand and watch for them. It is particularly important to consider the possibility of demonization when several of these symptoms show up together.

And there is another reason why we need to be aware of these symptoms: Recognizing the symptoms demons produce is crucial to discovering their names. We will discover why this is important in the next chapter.

14

What Demons' Names Reveal

L ooking at the symptoms of possible demonization can be confusing and discouraging. There is nothing that is unmistakably "supernatural" about any of the symptoms we looked at in thc last chapter. Often when a teen withdraws from friends and family there are obvious reasons. We hardly need demons to explain the behavior of hostile and angry people or an immoral lifestyle. And there are perfectly natural reasons for most illnesses, even the mysterious and chronic ones. There are even psychological causes for the epidemic of self-mutilation (cutting) we see increasingly among adolescent girls and young women today.

Two Important Things to Remember

It would be so much easier if the symptoms of demonization fit into a unique checklist, and we could confidently go down the list and say of one thing, "This is natural," and of another, "That is demonic." Unfortunately, that is not possible. Still, it is possible to identify the presence of demons in a person's life with certainty.

The first thing we need to understand is that demons do not create the symptoms that point to their presence. What demons do is hitchhike on problems that are already present, to exacerbate or magnify the symptoms.

An individual with a temper might open himself to demonization and find that his anger escalates into almost uncontrollable rage. A person who is subject to depression might find the depression deepening into suicidal despair. In such cases the presence of a temper or of depression gave demons a foothold, which they exploited to make the victim's problem worse.

What gives demons entry in the first place? Such things as unforgiveness, habitual sin, involvement in the occult, the lingering effects of past traumas—all provide points of entry for evil spirits.

So while the symptoms discussed in chapter 13 need not indicate demonization, extreme expression of those symptoms is more likely to indicate the active presence of evil spirits, and it suggests we should take additional steps.

A second thing to remember is that one of the gifts of the Holy Spirit is discernment of spirits. This is a gift that I do not have. I have, however, ministered alongside an individual who can sense the presence of evil and "read" evil spirits accurately. On one occasion we went to the home of a woman, living alone, who was visibly upset by objects moving by themselves in her bedroom and what she described as "a darkness." As we went through the house room by room, my teammate sensed no evil presences. But when we entered the woman's bedroom she sensed something there. "Quick," my companion said. "He's a minor one, but he's about to go for help."

I quickly commanded the spirit in Jesus' name to leave the home, never to return, and to enlist no other spirit to come to the home. My companion told me the spirit was gone, and the woman never again had a sense of a dark supernatural presence in her home.

This story illustrates the value of having the support of a person with the gift of discernment when dealing with evil spirits. One with such a proven gift can be a great aid in confirming demonization. But there are many times when such a helper simply is not available. How then can we tell whether or not a person displaying suspicious symptoms is demonized?

At this point we need to recognize the importance of demons' names.

Discovering Demons' Names

I suspect that all demons have personal names. Once in a great while a demon might reveal that personal name, such as the name Shabaz claimed by one demon, but this is extremely unusual.

Yet it is important if we are to conquer demons to know their names and use them. The names demons seem to go by are functional names. We see an example of this in an incident recorded in Mark 9.

When Jesus saw that a crowd was running to the scene, he rebuked the evil spirit. "You deaf and mute spirit," he said, "I command you, come out of him and never enter him again."

Mark 9:25

In this case Jesus addressed the evil spirit by name. And the spirit's name, Deaf and Mute, was that of the symptoms he produced.

The practice of naming persons by the work they do has a long tradition in many languages. Taylor, Farmer, Smith, Brewer and many other common names have roots in occupations going back to the Middle Ages. Similarly, we today know and name demons by their occupations, by the evil works they do within human beings. So Jesus' addressing, naming, this evil spirit as "you deaf and mute spirit" hardly is surprising.

If we understand how evil spirits can be named, we can expose them and remove them. Demons do not want to be exposed. They want to hide away inside the personality of the person they have entered and operate in secret. Even those who cannot get inside us want to whisper words of doubt or discouragement or fear in our ears. They especially do not want a believer who understands the power of Jesus to be able to name them.

This is why knowing their names is important. Demons can often avoid responding to a general command, such as, "Demon, come out." There is no certainty about to whom the exorcist is speaking, and, thus, the demon relies on a technicality and does not feel that he has to respond. This is especially true when several demons are present in an individual—a situation that is much more common than demonization by a single evil spirit.

Thus, it is important to address a demon you intend to send out by name, so the demon has no excuse for failing to respond to your command.

It is here that it becomes helpful to recognize the symptoms sketched in the preceding chapter. And this means that we need to get information that will help us understand just what the evil spirits are doing in a victim's life. If we understand the symptoms experienced by the demonized individual, we can usually name the evil spirit.

Let's look at some examples.

Thirty-two-year-old Jeff confides to us that he is upset at almost losing control when angry at his children. He tells us that he tries to stay calm, but he is easily irritated and has always had a hot temper. Somehow his children keep doing things that annoy him and set him off. He is becoming concerned that he might do something to hurt them.

This certainly sounds like demonization. So the first thing we do is to jot down some possible names by which demons in his life might be identified. Perhaps we jot down three: Anger, Fury, Rage.

The chances are in this case that a demon, if present, will operate under one of these names. The chances are even greater that more than one demon is involved. So we add the names of possibly associated demons: Annoyance, Irritation, Resentment.

Twenty-one-year-old Linda says that she is experiencing deep depression and has begun to cut herself. Talking with Linda we learn that the depression began when she was seventeen and had sex with a boy she was dating. He quickly went on to other girls. But Linda felt guilty and ashamed. About six months later she realized she was depressed, and as the depression deepened she began the cutting.

Again, this sounds like possible demonization, although we realize that there might be other psychological causes. When we learn that Linda has been getting counseling, with no obvious results, demonization seems more likely.

Our first step in dealing with Linda is to jot down names under which any demons present might be operating. As she talks, we make mental notes or jot down Guilt, Shame, Depression. And, sensitive to feelings she does not mention, we add Self-Loathing and Self-Hatred as possible demonic influencers.

Forty-year-old Jack confesses that he has a problem with pornography. He is happily married, has a good job, goes to church regularly and has been able to overcome other temptations. But pornography has him hooked, and he cannot seem to break its bonds.

As Jack talks we jot down likely names of any demons who might be involved in Jack's vulnerability to pornography. We jot down Pornography, of course. But we add: Lust, Desire and Covetousness to our list of possible names.

Now, in none of the situations described above is demonization *necessarily* involved. All that any of these situations might call for is a good counselor skilled in psychotherapy, or perhaps a pastor who can help someone like Linda find grace and forgiveness. But in many situations like these three, demonization will be involved.

And we will be aware of the situation simply because we know the person. It is most likely that we will know something about the situation through a personal relationship with the individual, or a relationship with a family member or a close friend of the troubled person. This is much more likely than a person becoming aware of his or her own demonization and seeking out a known deliverance minister. God may well have placed you near the demonized person so that you can be his agent for freedom.

The consequence is that anyone—people like you and me— might be called on to confront and to conquer demons in the name of Jesus. If we are called on, we will need to use the names of the demons present.

Treading Gently

For many victims, even the suggestion that part of their problem could be caused by a demon is frightening. Others will already sense an evil presence that troubles them, whether or not they recognize it as an evil spirit. In either case, we need to raise the possibility of demonization in a calm, matter-of-fact way. Most people will pick up our attitude. If we seem relaxed and unruffled when we raise the possibility of demonic involvement, it will be much easier for the victim to consider the possibility.

The chances are that we will already know the person well enough to recognize some of the symptoms that point to demonization. If we are uncertain about his or her symptoms, we will need to ask the individual to tell us a little more about the things that trouble him or her. What is most upsetting about his or her life just now? As you listen, jot down mentally or on a slip of paper key words that help identify possible demonic presences. As you question your friend or family member, do so with curiosity and concern, and without shock or judgment. And as you talk together, ask the Holy Spirit to guide you and alert you to any evil spirits that have a grip on your friend or loved one.

When you have a list of possible names, you are finally ready to find out—for sure—if what is going on in the person's life really is demonization.

15

Confirming Demonization

I might have given the impression in the preceding chapters that it is difficult to confirm a suspicion of demonization. If so, I apologize, because it really is not difficult at all. Two stories that we have studied from the book of Luke demonstrate why.

> *Jesus is in a synagogue teaching. Unexpectedly, a man in the congregation jumps up and the evil spirit cries out, "What do You want with us, Jesus of Nazareth?"*

> *Jesus steps ashore and is met by a demonized man. The man cries out, "What do You want with me, Son of the Most High God?" Jesus then asks the demon, "What is your name?" And the demon responds, "Legion."*

In the first case apparently there were no outward signs of demonization until the demon, terrified at the presence of Jesus, cried out. In the second case all the symptoms of demonization were present. But what is significant for us is that in both cases, the onlookers knew demons were present *because the evil spirits spoke and told them.*

This is exactly how we confirm today whether a person's symptoms are caused by demons or not: If the demons do not reveal themselves on their own, we can make them tell us that they are present. We do this by using the names of suspected demons and commanding them to acknowledge and reveal their presence.

Before we look at the specifics of commanding demons to acknowledge their presence, I want to explain what to do if a demon "acts out." How do we deal with this showy behavior?

When to "Rebuke" an Evil Spirit

If you have seen movies like *The Exorcist* or watched deliverance ministries on TV, you might get the idea that sometimes demons act out, which, by the way, easily confirms demonic presence. There is biblical precedent for this. When Jesus cast out a demon from the child whose story is told in Luke, we are told that "the demon threw [the boy] to the ground in a convulsion" (Luke 9:42).

Note that this was not how the demonization was discovered. The child had already been diagnosed as the victim of an evil spirit (see Luke 9:39). The convulsion was the last vindictive act of the demon before Jesus evicted him. When Jesus "rebuked the evil spirit" (verse 42), the power of the demon over the child was broken.

This is helpful for us to remember. Under pressure, a demon may try to act out. Some books by exorcists tell of people falling to the floor and wriggling like snakes, others of slight women suddenly so strong that the exorcists' teams cannot hold them down. Acting out in these and other ways might well be a demonic strategy, not only to further harm a victim but also to distract us as we prepare to cast the demon out.

If we should encounter something like this, we are to follow Jesus' example and rebuke the evil spirit. That is, we are, in the name of Jesus, to tell the evil spirit to stop. He is to do nothing to harm his victim, and he is to stop acting out in any way.

Again, I suspect that one of the reasons demons sometimes try this strategy is to distract, or perhaps to frighten, the person who is about to cast them out. We need to remember when confronting an evil spirit that the demon is not in charge. *We are!*

Let's remember that we can rebuke evil spirits who try such strategies and in the name of Jesus command them to stop!

The Confirming Admission

If it is not readily apparent, we can confirm whether or not a person is demonized. We can force demons to tell us that they are present. Simply put, we do this by using their names and commanding them to speak through, or speak to, their victims.

Demons "Speaking Through"

In "speaking through," the demon is given permission to use his victim's organs of speech. In many cases the voice in which the demon speaks is dramatically different from the normal voice of the individual. Even when the voice is similar, there are differences in tone and expression that make it obvious to observers that the person herself or himself is not the one who is speaking.

This experience can be frightening to the demonized person, who suddenly becomes aware that someone or something is using his voice. It is important to ask the person if he will give the demon permission to speak through him.

Some might dismiss this phenomenon as an expression of Dissociative Identity Disorder. In DID an individual has a number of "alters," or multiple personalities. When an alter is in control there can be a significant difference in personality and voice, just as with demons. In many cases of DID, the main personality is not aware of what the alters are saying or doing. Other individuals who have DID are "co-conscious" and *do* hear the alters thinking and speaking. In such cases the individual generally can tell the difference between alters and demons.

You can see the importance of treading carefully whenever DID is suspected. We must not try to "cast out" an alternative personality nor let a harmful demon stay entrenched.

Demons "Speaking To"

When we command a demon to "speak to" the demonized person, the evil spirit communicates to the victim directly. Often words or ideas form in the demonized person's mind, which he or she is aware are not his or her own. We speak directly to the demon, and the demonized person can relay what the evil spirit is revealing.

In my experience, most people from whom I have cast out demons prefer to have demons speak to, rather than through them. This has not inhibited in any way the identification and expulsion of any demons present.

One woman I prayed with sensed the demon as a dragon, nesting in the left side of her chest. As I named it and commanded it to leave, she felt as if it were tearing loose from her body. Suddenly relaxing, she told me, "It's gone."

We will take a closer look at the process of conquering demons in the next part of this book, which lays out a pattern you can follow if you are called on to conquer demons in Jesus' name. For now, it is important to remember that we can and will confirm demonization by compelling any evil spirits to reveal themselves to their victims and to us.

Summary of Part 4

Defining Demonization

Demonization is the presence of a demon or evil spirit within the personality of an individual. Just how demons attach themselves to humans, and how they exercise their influence within a victim's personality, is not really understood. The gospels, however, picture demons as "in" their victims, for again and again the text tells us that Jesus cast evil spirits "out." It is also clear from the gospels that the majority of the demonized were believers. While the case of the Syrophoenician woman's daughter (see Mark 7) indicates that pagans can be demonized, Jesus' primary ministry was to God's Old Testament people.

Many of the incidents recorded in the gospels depict physical symptoms of demonization. The story of the demoniac of Gadara points to symptoms in a number of areas, ranging from the physical to social, moral, interpersonal, psychological and mental. We need to be aware of symptoms, for they can help us identify the names of any demons who might be present. Demons operate under and answer to functional names. That is, a demon is named by the evil work he is doing within a demonized person. Thus, for instance, demon Rage enhances anger; demon Lust stimulates evil desires; etc.

In ministering to a possibly demonized individual, we need to identify the symptoms and make a list of possible names of the demons who might be amplifying the symptoms we observe.

We use the names of suspected demons when we command demons to acknowledge and reveal their presence. Demons seek to remain hidden, but when addressed by name and called out in the name of Jesus, demons will speak either through or to a demonized person. We want to rebuke other ways demons express their presence by acting out, remembering that we, not the demons, are in charge in this confrontation.

When we have identified and confirmed the presence of evil spirits in the life of a demonized person, we can go on to conquer the demons and cast them out.

Part 5

The Conquest

16

In the Name of Jesus

We can sense the enthusiasm of the 72 Jesus had sent out to carry His message to the towns of Galilee. Bursting with excitement, they returned and reported to Jesus, "Lord, even the demons submit to us in your name" (Luke 10:17).

This simple report sums up four realities that we need to keep in mind when we are called on to minister to a demonized individual, or when demons encroach upon our daily lives.

Jesus Is Lord

This is the first and foundational reality to count on as we confront evil spirits. The theme of Christ's Lordship is pre-eminent in the New Testament.

- Christ has been raised from the dead, and is now in the heavenly realms, "far above all rule and authority, power and dominion, and every title that can be given," and God has "placed all things under his feet" (Ephesians 1:21–22).

- Jesus is "the image of the invisible God" and "all things were created by and for him" (Colossians 1:15–16).

- He is "the beginning and the firstborn from the dead, so that in everything he might have the supremacy" (Colossians 1:18).

- Jesus is the "heir of all things," through whom God "made the universe." He is the "exact representation of [God's] being, sustaining all things by his powerful word" (Hebrews 1:2–3).

- Although Christ, as God the Son, was "in very nature God," He humbled himself to die on a cross, only to be raised to new life and exalted "to the highest place . . . that at the name of Jesus every knee should bow . . . and every tongue confess that Jesus Christ is Lord" (Philippians 2:6, 9–11).

As Lord, Jesus is supreme in all things, and all things have been placed "under His feet," an idiom meaning "under His authority." It is in His name that you and I will cast out demons, for Jesus is supreme.

The Demons Submit

This is the second reality that so thrilled the original 72. Throughout history, supernatural beings, whatever they were called, had been held in awe and feared. Now, unexpectedly, demons were submitting to these followers of Jesus.

This is even truer for you and me today. Colossians 2 tells us that in His death Jesus forgave us all our sins and made us "alive with Christ" (Colossians 2:13). The passage goes on to state that Jesus also "disarmed the powers and authorities" and "made a public spectacle of them, triumphing over them by the cross" (Colossians 2:15). Remember that *powers* and *authorities* were terms used in the first century to describe supernatural beings, those very beings we call demons and evil spirits. At the cross these spiritual forces of evil were not only defeated; they were disarmed.

There is an important truth underlined in this passage. God has always had the raw power needed to crush evil wherever it occurs in His universe. But might does not make right. God had to establish a moral basis to extend forgiveness to the human beings He has always loved, even though we have rebelled against Him and become evil ourselves. By taking on Himself the punishment due us, Jesus established the moral basis for our forgiveness (see Romans 3:24–26).

But there was another issue. As sinners, we had become vulnerable to Satan and his demons. In the words of 2 Timothy 2:26, we had been "taken . . . captive" by the devil "to do his will." In the cross God not only won forgiveness for us, He also "disarmed" Satan, breaking His power over us. Paul goes on to say that God "made a public spectacle of them." The reference is to the practice in the Roman empire of voting a victorious general a public triumph, in which he and his legions marched through the streets of Rome, followed by the disarmed and disgraced enemy. Making a public spectacle of the defeated foe both humiliated them and added to the glory of the victor.

Spiritually speaking, the forced submission of demonic powers and evil spirits exposes them as a defeated enemy and glorifies Jesus, who won the victory for us on His cross. And the fact that we who had once been Satan's captives now can command those who were once our captors emphasizes the total victory of God over evil. Satan and his demons have not yet been dispatched. But they have been defeated and must submit.

Let's never forget that these beings we once might have feared have been defeated and disarmed by Jesus. The demons submit because they must, for the resurrected Jesus truly is Lord.

The Demons Submit *to Us*

This was said in awe and wonder. Not one of the 72 who returned after casting out demons had the personal power to force demons to submit. They were ordinary people, just as you and I are ordinary people. In ourselves we have no special powers, no intrinsic authority to exercise in commanding demons. This, too, is something we must always keep in mind when confronting evil spirits. We come to this ministry humbly, sharing the awe and wonder that, through Jesus, evil spirits do submit when we command them in Jesus' name.

In Jesus' Name

Names have special significance in Scripture. They affirm something specific about the nature of the person or thing named. So when we pray "in Jesus' name" we are not only expressing confidence in Jesus' promise that prayers in His name will be answered, but also affirming that what we are praying for is in harmony with His nature and motives. Yet something different is expressed in the report from the 72 that demons submitted to them "in Your name."

Jesus once was approached by a Roman centurion who asked Him to heal a servant lying at home in terrible suffering. Jesus offered to go and heal him, but the centurion objected. He was not worthy to have Jesus in his home. So if Jesus would just say the word, his servant would be healed. The centurion went on to explain. "I myself am a man under authority, with soldiers under me. I tell this one, 'Go,' and he goes; and to that one, 'Come,' and he comes" (Matthew 8:9). The explanation may seem obscure to us, but it was clear to the centurion and to Jesus. The reason this military officer could order about the soldiers under him was because he himself was "a man under authority." That is, he would be obeyed not because of who he was as an individual, but because he was acting under an authority that could be traced back to the emperor himself. The centurion did not expect the soldiers to obey him because he was a nice person, or because they liked him, or for any personal quality. He expected the soldiers to obey because he was a superior officer who derived his authority from those above him. It was clear to the centurion that Jesus spoke with the authority of God above, so Jesus could simply "say the word," and his desperately ill servant would be healed.

It is the same as the police officer of our own day who calls out, "Stop, in the name of the law." He is not saying, "I, Pete Jones, tell you to stop." Pete Jones does not mean anything. But when he says, "Stop, in the name of the law," Pete Jones is acting in his capacity as an officer of the law, and all the authority of the state is behind his command.

That is what happens when we command evil spirits in the name of Jesus. If I were to try to command an evil spirit in the name of Larry Richards, the demon would most certainly ignore or ridicule me. Or attack me. In myself, I am nothing to evil spirits beyond a potential victim. But when I command evil spirits in the name of Jesus, I am not speaking for myself. I am speaking with authority that comes from and is backed up by all that Jesus is. And Jesus is Lord.

In the next chapter we will begin to work through what happens when we confront an evil spirit who is demonizing a human being we are called to free. But our first priority must be to arm ourselves with confidence in Jesus. Soon we will be able to say with the 72, "Lord, even the demons submit to us in Your name!"

17

Clearing the Way

In an earlier chapter I sketched briefly the case of Linda, a fictional 21-year-old who is struggling with depression. Here is what I wrote about her.

Twenty-one-year-old Linda says that she is experiencing deep depression and has begun to cut herself. Talking with Linda we learn that the depression began when she was seventeen and had sex with a boy she was dating. He quickly went on to other girls. But Linda felt guilty and ashamed. About six months later she realized she was depressed, and as the depression deepened she began the cutting.

Again, this sounds like possible demonization, although we realize that there might be other psychological causes. When we learn that Linda has been getting counseling, with no obvious results, demonization seems more likely.

Our first step in dealing with Linda is to jot down names under which any demons present might be operating. As she talks, we make mental notes or jot down Guilt, Shame,

Depression. And, sensitive to feelings she does not mention, we add Self-Loathing and Self-Hatred as possible demonic influencers.

After listening compassionately to what Linda has shared, we feel led to explore with her the possibility of demonization. This chapter will follow that conversation. Each conversation with a possibly demonized individual will be different. There is no formula to follow. So we need to invite the Holy Spirit to take charge of each conversation and to guide all we say and do. But while there is no formula, we do have a general idea of what we need to do to clear the way to deal with any demons present.

Here are a few steps that can lead to freedom.

Introduce the Possibility

This is often the first step. Usually the best way to approach the question of demonization is a direct one. Speaking in a conversational voice, we might say, "Linda, sometimes there's more involved in the kind of depression that you've been experiencing. I mean, sometimes there's something evil, something supernatural behind what's been troubling you. Have you ever felt that way?"

Often a person who has been demonized will have some awareness of an evil presence. But even if Linda says, "No, I've never felt that way," we can continue to explain.

We might say, "You know that Jesus cast out demons that made people sick or disabled them? It's possible that a demon might be oppressing you and making your depression worse."

Again, whether Linda responds positively or thinks the notion of demons is mere superstition, we can continue. It is important not to argue or try to convince Linda of something she does not yet believe in. So we can say something like, "I don't know whether Satan or evil spirits are making your depression worse. But I'd really love to see you free of any negative spiritual forces if they are there."

Notice that in bringing up the possibility of demonization we have not asked Linda to agree with us. We have been careful to express our beliefs while respecting hers. At the same time, we have said plainly what we want. If there is any supernatural force that is making her depression worse, we want to see Linda set free.

Gain Cooperation

At this point we can ask her directly, "Would you like to get rid of any evil spirits that might be troubling you?"

If you have a good relationship with Linda, she might quickly say, "Yes." But many other responses are possible. "No, that's scary. I don't even want to think about evil spirits and demons." Or, "How can you possibly help me?"

The truthful answer is, "Linda, it's not what I can do. It's what Jesus can do. Just as He freed people in the gospels who were oppressed by evil spirits, He is able to free people today. If there are any evil spirits making your depression worse, Jesus can free you."

Linda might or might not be a Christian. If she is not a believer, we could say, "I realize you don't believe that Jesus can make a difference right now. But if you're willing to give Him a chance, I'll pray for you and be right here to help you."

At this point Linda could refuse our help. In that case, we tell her we understand, ask if it is all right if we pray for her, and tell her that whenever she wants to find out if Jesus can free her, she is welcome to ask us.

It is most likely that, if Linda is a believer, and even if she is not, she will be willing to take the next step with you. We want always to respect Linda as a person who can and must make her own choices. If Linda is demonized, the demon will probably raise all sorts of objections in her mind, but Linda still has the freedom to make her own choice. And our prayer that the Holy Spirit will take control of the conversation means that God is actively countering any demonic influence.

In most cases people will agree when we ask, "Are you willing to give Him a chance?" We have gained their cooperation. This is important, for exorcism is typically a cooperative process.

Preview the Process

We do not want Linda to be surprised or frightened by anything that happens. In fact, we want the process of identifying and casting out any demons to feel as natural as possible. We can help by maintaining a calm and matter-of-fact tone of voice as we describe what is going to happen.

We tell Linda that first we will just chat for a while about her depression, about when it started, about anything that makes it seem worse and how being plunged into depression makes her feel. We explain that while we are talking together we might take down notes that could help identify any evil spirits that might be oppressing her.

We also explain at some point that we will speak directly to any evil spirits that might be there, and command them to reveal themselves. We tell her that this is nothing like the supposed exorcisms we see in movies. Any spirits present will simply speak in Linda's mind or, if she gives them permission, use her voice to speak out loud.

We tell Linda that often more than one demon or evil spirit will join up to make a person's life miserable. If we find that demons have been making her depression worse, we will make sure each and every one is identified and sent out of her life.

Clear the Way

There are times when we will want to clear away obstacles to exorcism. If Linda is a believer, we will want to be sure she has confessed any sins that led to the depression. There may also be anger at the boy who used her and left, or a sense of guilt over the practice of cutting.

We want to encourage her to confess any sins she is aware of and to forgive individuals who have hurt her. Unconfessed sin and unforgiveness seem to give evil spirits a particularly strong position; demons claim that these conditions give them the legal right to be present in the person's life. This claim of a legal right is, in essence, fiction. Even if the person has engaged in occult activity and invited the spirit into her life, repentance and repudiation of that invitation is possible. This, like confession of sin and the choice to forgive, weakens any demonic strongholds and brings the person who has been troubled by demons into that closer relationship with Jesus that will be so important in resisting future demonic attacks. There is no question that at some point we will deal with issues like these, along with distorted beliefs Linda might have about God and herself.

There are situations in which it is best to deal with these issues after the evil spirits have been driven out rather than before. This is another reason why we rely totally on the Holy Spirit and seek to remain open to His leading. Only the Holy Spirit knows which approach is best for a given individual.

Some in deliverance ministry will present the Gospel to an unsaved person before driving out demons. Others tend to present the Gospel after the individual has experienced the power of Jesus to overcome demons. Again, what we do in a given situation will vary, and we need to follow the leading of the Spirit as He guides us.

18

Confronting the Demon

At this point we are not sure that demons are present. We know they might be. And we know that if they are present, they want to remain hidden. So our first step is to command the demons present to reveal themselves.

Some like to begin this process of confronting demons by reading or quoting Scripture. I frequently find myself using passages I quoted in chapter 16, along with passages from Revelation that describe Christ's final triumph. I do not usually plan when to introduce Scripture, but I find I am often led to do it. It is good to remind the demons of who Jesus is, of Satan's decisive defeat at Calvary and of their destiny. Whether or not this has the effect of weakening the demons' resolve I do not know. But I am often led to do this at some point during the process.

As we saw in chapter 14, it is important to address demons by their functional names. As Linda's presenting problem is her depression, it is likely there is at least one demon named

Depression. So we begin by commanding, "Depression, in the name of Jesus, reveal yourself." It might take repeated commands before the reluctant demon reveals himself. As I noted earlier, demons can speak through a demonized person's voice or to the individual, forming mental impressions of words or images.

It might also be that the demon who is exacerbating Linda's condition is not Depression, but goes by the name of Despair or Self-Loathing. If we do not gain a response from Depression, we need to direct our command to another demon. These are the names we jotted down as we developed insight into Linda's problems, along with likely demonic influencers.

As a demon within Linda grudgingly reveals himself, the discovery that someone or something is present within her may shock or frighten her, despite your preparation of her for this experience. We remind Linda that any presence she feels is subject to Jesus.

As soon as an evil spirit is sensed, we give this command: "Demon of depression, you will do nothing to harm, frighten or influence Linda in any way. Nor are you to touch anyone or anything she cares about." We command the evil spirit not to manifest in any frightening way, but simply to answer our questions and follow our orders.

Questioning Demons

It may seem tempting, once we have established contact with an actual demon, to probe for information about all sorts of things we are curious about in the spirit world. This is unwise. Demons, like Satan, are liars, and we can hardly trust what they tell us. Most important, the authority Jesus gives us is the authority to cast out demons in His name. We have no authority to seek information on the spirit world. Scripture has revealed what God wants us to know about that realm, and we are to be satisfied with that revelation.

There are, however, questions that are directly related to freeing Linda that we do need to ask. These are:

What other demons are present with you?

What are their names?

Who is the lead demon?

This last question is particularly important. The world of demons is rigidly hierarchical, with lower-ranking demons taking orders from higher-ranking demons. The lead demon in a person will often resist being identified and order the demon we are speaking to not to identify him.

One friend of mine simply commands any demons other than the one he is speaking to not to hear what is being said until he gives them permission to listen. This seems to relieve the pressure on the demon we are talking to, and he will much more readily identify the lead demon and any others who are present.

At this point we need to call out the lead demon and deal directly with him.

Let me say this again: While trying to gain information about the spirit world is out of order, there are appropriate questions that can help free Linda from her demonization. We might ask the lead demon,

How long have demons been in Linda's life?

What opened the door that let you in?

What right, if any, do you claim you have to be there?

We might also ask,

What lies have you told Linda about herself?

What else have you done to oppress her?

Demons seem to be quite legalistic and will often insist that they have a right to be in a person's life. That "legal right" might be because Linda, unaware of a demon's true nature, cried out to the demonic for help. It might be because of some specific or repeated sin that gave the demons a foothold. All too often today individuals are seduced into inviting an occult "spirit guide" into their lives. Once we have identified the entry point, and the legal right that the demons claim, we need to lead Linda to confess to the Lord any sin involved, and to repudiate verbally any choices or actions that led to the demonization.

With the demons' legal ground removed, we can continue with the exorcism. And with the information we have gained, we can teach Linda how to protect herself against subsequent demonization.

Expelling the Demons

One of my friends who has extensive experience casting out evil spirits asks the demonized person to visualize a box, and then orders the demons present to get into the box. When all the demons have followed his orders, he closes and locks the box, and asks God to send angels to carry the box of demons to Jesus to deal with as He chooses. In most cases the demonized person can "see" the demons get into the box, and some will "see" the angels carrying the box away.

Almost any such visualization technique will be effective. We might, for instance, ask the person we are freeing to visualize giving the lead demon sets of handcuffs. Then we order the lead demon to handcuff each of the demons that are present to each other, forming a chain of cuffed demons. In

Jesus' name we command the lead demon to make sure that he and all the demons present in the person are now chained together. We might now ask God to send angels, or we could simply command the chained demons to report to Jesus for Him to do whatever He chooses with them.

Such visualizations are not necessary to expel the demons. We can simply command them, by name, to leave the demonized individual. This is what Christ did, as in Mark 9:25. There, as we have noted, Jesus dealt with an evil spirit by commanding, "You deaf and mute spirit, . . . come out of him and never enter him again." There will be times when you will cast out an evil spirit just as simply and straightforwardly.

Note that in the gospel story "the spirit shrieked, convulsed him violently and came out" (Mark 9:26). This response of the demon was convincing evidence that the demon had been there and was now gone; the visualization performs the same function. The demonized person recognizes that evil spirits had tormented him, and has witnessed them leaving. And the casting out of spirits generally provides a sense of peace and relief, as if a heavy weight has been removed.

But casting out the demons is not the end of deliverance ministry. In a sense, it is the beginning.

19

Bolting the Doors

In Luke 11 Jesus tells a significant story, one that we need to take seriously when ministering to anyone who has been demonized.

"When an evil spirit comes out of a man, it goes through arid places seeking rest and does not find it. Then it says, 'I will return to the house I left.' When it arrives, it finds the house swept clean and put in order. Then it goes and takes seven other spirits more wicked than itself, and they go in and live there. And the final condition of that man is worse than the first."

Luke 11:24–26

This story Jesus tells reminds us that demons are eager to be inside human beings. Once a demon has experienced residence in a human personality, any other state seems "arid" and leaves the demon restless. A demon who has been cast out wants to return. And should it find the personality (house) "swept clean and put in order" . . . but empty . . . it recruits more demons to join it in the invasion of the individual's personality. Jesus' illustration is an uncomfortable one. It reminds us that just because evil spirits have been expelled from our lives, we are not necessarily immune to future demonization. At the same time, the illustration is a source of both guidance and hope. In it, Jesus points the way to make our freedom from demonization permanent.

Swept Clean

On the one hand, sweeping clean might refer to the original expulsion of the demons who had been present. But certainly more is implied. There were things in the now freed person's life that opened the door for a demonic invasion. As we noted earlier, such things as unforgiveness, habitual sin, involvement in the occult and the lingering effects of past traumas can all provide points of entry for evil spirits.

It is important to help a person from whom we have just expelled one or more demons to identify and deal with these entry points. Incidents that have made her bitter and angry need to be identified, and the persons involved forgiven. Habitual sins need to be confessed to God and repudiated. Ungodly thought patterns need to be replaced. No one whose life and thoughts are filled with such junk can expect to keep out evil spirits.

We also need to be aware that many of Linda's thoughts and reactions are deeply ingrained. She is likely to find herself thinking in old ways and be tempted to react as she used to. She might even seem to hear the demons' voices urging her on. When she becomes aware of old ways of thinking and feeling, she can exercise the authority Jesus gives all His people and command any demons that are troubling her to stop, in Jesus' name.

Taking steps like these can be difficult for someone who has been demonized, and a good professional counselor can help the person deal with her issues and find further healing. At the very least she needs to build a relationship with one or more persons who will pray for her and hold her accountable as she seeks to clear away ungodly thoughts, attitudes and practices.

Set in Order

After a person has been freed from demons, he or she will need to rebuild. Linda, who has felt guilt and shame over her failure as a seventeen-year-old, will need to accept Jesus' forgiveness, and to forgive herself as well as the boy who so callously exploited her.

She will need to focus consciously on the positive things in her life, even making a list daily of things to praise God for. Linda will also need to begin to see herself as God sees her, as an individual who is precious to Him—so precious Jesus was willing to give His life for her. As Linda's beliefs about herself and her attitudes change, the self-loathing and the cutting will gradually recede.

Again, remember that these changes, like the process of sweeping the house clean, take time. Linda will definitely need additional help and support, more help and support than your ministry team is able to provide alone. So it is really important for Linda to have relationships with others who will love her and support her as changes take place.

In some cases a person like Linda will need the help of a trained psychotherapist. In perhaps most cases someone like Linda will need the support of a small group of Christians who meet regularly to pray for and encourage each other, a small group where Linda and others can be real in sharing their struggles as well as their victories. Without such support most people will find it extremely difficult to sweep their lives clean, or to set their lives in order.

Who Lives There?

It seems almost shocking, after Jesus' words about the house (the life) swept clean and set in order, to hear Him say that the original evil spirit "takes seven other spirits more wicked than itself, and they go in and live there." At least it seems shocking, until we realize the implications of Jesus' warning. The person who was demonized worked hard to sweep his life clean of those things that attracted demons. And he worked hard to set his life in order. But when the demons returned, they found the core of the individual's personality empty.

In His Last Supper discourse, Jesus told His disciples that if anyone loves Him and obeys His teaching, "My Father will love him, and we will come to him and make our home with him" (John 14:23). The secret of the Christian life is not reform, as important as that is. The secret is personal relationship with Jesus, God the Father and the Holy Spirit. God is eager to fill our lives with Himself, and a life that has been set in order, swept clean *and filled with Jesus* is not a welcome home for demons.

It is certainly true that we can also cast demons out of those who do not know Jesus. But before such persons leave the ministry time, we need both to warn them and to encourage them. It was Jesus who expelled the demons that oppressed them. They have experienced His power. Now this same Jesus invites them to trust Him for the forgiveness of sins and adoption into God's own family. This same Jesus will come into their lives. And as they learn to live in relationship with Jesus, He will protect them from evil spirits who are eager to return.

Summary of Part 5

The Conquest

Jesus holds supreme power in the universe. At Calvary, Christ not only paid for our sin but decisively defeated Satan. Today we are authorized to act in Jesus' name to cast out demons, thus freeing those whom evil spirits are oppressing.

When ministering to a demonized individual, we introduce the possibility of supernatural involvement in his problems, and seek to gain his cooperation in removing any evil spirits. We try to help the individual deal with issues that demons claim as a legal basis for their presence, such as unconfessed sin. We then confront the demons we suspect to be present by name, ordering them to reveal themselves by speaking in or through the demonized person.

We identify the lead demon and learn all we can about others who might be present. When we believe we have identified all the demons present, we expel them and send them to Jesus to be dealt with as He chooses.

Because we realize the demons will try to return, we counsel and help the freed individual both to clean and to set his life in order. But most important, we encourage a faith commitment to Jesus, and do all we can to help him find relationships within which he can experience growth in his Christian life.

Part 6

Living Victoriously

20

Three Guidelines for a Victorious Christian Life

What, really, is a "victorious Christian life"?

If we look to Jesus for the answer, we discover quickly that it is not a life of spiritual highs with no spiritual lows. It is not a comfortable life, a life without stress or struggle. In John 15:20 Jesus warns His disciples, "If they persecuted me [and they certainly did!], they will persecute you also." The victorious Christian is not always popular with the crowds. Peter reminds us that many will abuse us because we no longer plunge with them into the same flood of dissipation (see 1 Peter 4:4). We Christians are not the ones praised on *Entertainment Tonight*. No, a victorious Christian life is very different from the "happy" life that people in most cultures think of as their right, rather than a privilege.

If I were to define a truly victorious Christian life, I would be tempted to say: It is living a human life just as Jesus did. It is a life lived in intimate fellowship with God the Father, ever responsive to His written Word and the promptings of the Holy Spirit.

This means no one can create a rule book for victorious Christian living. Each believer is a unique individual, living in his or her own unique network of circumstances and relationships. But while there is no rule book for those who yearn to experience a victorious Christian life, there are guidelines. Here are three.

The First Guideline

Focus on and be aware of the presence of Christ in your life. There are different ways of expressing and deepening that awareness. One of these certainly is prayer, a practice of Jesus we see in the gospels. Another is learning more and more about the God who loves us as He reveals Himself to us in Scripture. Another is to develop relationships with fellow believers where we share our lives and encourage each other to follow Jesus more closely.

Some would twist these guidelines into rules, such as one must start the day with a thirty-minute devotional. There is nothing wrong with such a practice, but we need to find our own ways of expressing and deepening our awareness of God's presence.

The Second Guideline

Nurture an interest in and concern for those around you. Peter picks up on this theme, writing, "Above all, love each other deeply" (1 Peter 4:8). Often simply listening with compassion as a person shares his or her struggles is the most important thing we can do. At other times, Peter points out, loving may involve going beyond listening and offering hospitality—that is, acting to help meet the pressing needs of another (see verse 9).

The New Testament gives clear pictures of the relationships we are to develop with our fellow Christians, from being careful not to take offense to forgiving those who hurt us. And the New Testament also calls us to show the same loving concern for those who have not yet come to know Jesus. What a privilege to wake up each morning, wondering what opportunities God will provide that day to show Christ's love in our relationship with others!

The Third Guideline

Accept your role as a warrior in God's invisible war with Satan. By this I do not mean that every Christian should expect to cast out demons, although any of us can. What I have in mind is something I pointed out early in noting that Christ came to destroy the works of the devil.

Satan is doing all he can to corrupt our thinking, our values and our culture, and in the process build his own kingdom of darkness. But in Jesus we have been rescued from the "dominion of darkness and brought into the kingdom of the Son he loves" (Colossians 1:13). As warriors in the invisible war, we are called not so much to attack expressions of Satan's activities but to expose them by living godly lives, always being ready to give the reason for the hope that is in us (see 1 Peter 3:15).

The amazing and wonderful truth is that we can and do experience victorious Christian living in the course of our very ordinary lives. The simplest layman can live in the awareness of Christ's presence and show love and concern for others, and, by doing so, can "overcome evil with good" (Romans 12:21).

The victorious Christian studies to know God's Word, realizing that God will have a specific word of guidance for us when we undergo our own trials. As we do meet and overcome these tests, both our commitment to God and our trust in Him are strengthened.

Jesus best summed up the secret to a victorious Christian life, telling His disciples, "I seek not to please myself but him who sent me" (John 5:30). If this is our goal, and we are committed heart and soul to seeking to please God, we will live a truly victorious Christian life.

Summary of Part 6

Living Victoriously

Nearly every element we have looked at in this book on offensive spiritual warfare, Jesus' way, is critical to victorious Christian living. There really is a cosmic struggle taking place between God and Satan, between good and evil. At the cross, where Jesus won our salvation, He defeated Satan decisively and confirmed His place of supreme power in the universe. Although the struggle goes on until Jesus' return, our personal relationship today with the Victor gives us the power to overcome not only Satan's demons but our own sinfulness and weaknesses.

We see the path to victory in our own lives in Jesus' responses to temptation. Like Christ, who met each temptation in His human nature, we today can know and understand God's Word, trust in the love that motivates all the Father does and be responsive to the guidance provided by the Holy Spirit.

Like Jesus, we are also called to a life of ministry to others. As we embody God's love of every person, in whatever setting God has placed us, we are doing Christ's work. We can expect opposition and misunderstanding, but in loving as Jesus loved, we participate in His victory over evil.

We may never be called on to cast demons out of those we come to love and to serve. But as we live our lives for others and concentrate on overcoming evil with good, we will experience a truly victorious, and fulfilling, Christian life.

Appendix

Jesus' Confrontations with Evil Spirits

Incidents of confrontation between Jesus and evil spirits are found throughout the gospels. Frequently the same incidents are reported in several gospels. Typically there are minor variations in the reports, as one writer includes information the others leave out, or as one focuses on a specific point. In this appendix we look at each confrontation, drawing insights from the reports each writer provides.

Here is a chart listing the parallel Scriptures discussed here.

Jesus Teaches about Demons

Matthew	Mark	Luke	John
4:1–11	1:12–13	4:1–13	
4:24			
8:16	1:32–34	4:40–41	
8:28–34	5:1–20	8:26–39	
9:32–33			
9:34			

Matthew	Mark	Luke	John
10:1–10	3:13–19	9:1–3	
12:22–32	3:20–30	11:14–23	
12:43–45		11:24–26	
15:21–28	7:24–30		
17:14–21	9:14–29	9:37–42	
25:41			
	1:21–28	4:31–37	
	3:11–12		
	9:38–41	9:49–50	
	16:9		
	16:14–20		
		6:18–19	
		7:18–23	
		10:1–24	
		13:10–17	
			7:19–20
			8:31–47
			10:19–21
			13:2
			13:26–30

The Temptation of Jesus (Matthew 4:1–11; Mark 1:12–13; Luke 4:1–13)

Then Jesus was led by the Spirit into the desert to be tempted by the devil.

Matthew 4:1

These passages, which deal with what is called the temptation of Christ, are discussed extensively in chapters 5 through 8 of this book. Yet there is an important point we need to emphasize. The text tells us that "Jesus was led by the Spirit into the desert to be tempted by the devil."

"Jesus was led by the Spirit into the desert"—It is clear that God intended Jesus to go through the temptation experience. We need to recognize that the troubles and challenges we face in life may result from a similar leading. Rather than assume God is angry with us about something, or that He has forgotten us, we need to recognize that the kind of temptation Jesus experienced might very well be the will of God for us. Like Jesus, God intends us to triumph in and through our temptations.

"to be tempted by the devil"—The word translated "tempted" is *peirazo*, which is more frequently translated "tested" or "test." A better translation of the above verse is that the Spirit did not lead Jesus into the wilderness to be tempted by Satan, but to be tested by him.

Whenever God tests us, His intent is that we should be "approved." The Greek word translated "approved" is *dokimos*, which is also translated "stood the test" and "tested and approved." The Lord sometimes leads us into situations where our trust or commitment is challenged. While Satan tries to use such experiences to alienate us from God, the Lord's intent is never to trip us. Rather, God is giving us the opportunity to demonstrate to Him, to ourselves and to the world how powerfully He is at work in our lives.

The classic example of such a test is provided by Abraham. Told by God to sacrifice his son Isaac, Abraham immediately set out for the place of sacrifice. Reaching it, Abraham was about to kill his son when the Lord stopped him and pointed out a ram tangled in a thicket. Abraham did offer a sacrifice, but it was the ram rather than Isaac.

Commenting on the Genesis 22 story, Hebrews 11:19 tells us that, since God had promised that Abraham's descendants would also be offspring of Isaac, "Abraham reasoned that God could raise the dead." Abraham's confidence in the promise God made to him about Isaac's future (see Genesis 22:18) enabled Abraham to pass this test and to demonstrate that his trust in the Lord was real and vital. What a comfort, when God leads us into difficult situations, to know that the test is intended to affirm us rather than expose our weaknesses! God intends for us to pass every test, as Jesus passed every test Satan could devise. The key to passing our tests and living victoriously is to place complete confidence in God and demonstrate that confidence by obedience to His Word.

Just Another Disease (Matthew 4:24)

> News about him [Jesus] spread all over Syria, and people brought to him all who were ill with various diseases, those suffering severe pain, the demon-possessed, those having seizures, and the paralyzed, and he healed them.
>
> Matthew 4:24

The Greek word for *demon-possessed* is *daimonizomai*, "demonized." The word *possessed* is not found in the Greek text. To call an individual "possessed" gives the unfortunate and erroneous impression that demons take control of an individual. In fact, a demonized person's experience will be influenced by the presence of a demon, yet the person will remain responsible and free to make his or her own choices. When quoting passages I will substitute *demonized* for *demon-possessed*.

"ill with various diseases"—The list of disabilities that follows illustrates what Matthew views as "diseases." It is significant that demonization appears on this list, alongside seizures, paralysis and severe pain. Here demonization is

clearly placed in the category of "illness" or "disease." One implication is that, while demonization is a condition that has a debilitating impact on humans, it is no more "unusual" than seizures or severe pain. No one today would argue that Christians are immune to illness or severe pain. By including demonization on this list, Matthew reminds us that believers are no more immune to demonization than to any illness or disease.

"and he healed them"—Jesus responded to these sufferers by healing them. Here the demonized, too, are restored to health (normalcy) by healing. The word translated "healed" is *iaomai*. It is one of five Greek words meaning "to heal, to cure or to restore to health." Strikingly, of the 82 times these words are found in the New Testament, 73 are found in the gospels and Acts. While miracles of healing were common in the ministry of Jesus and to a lesser extent in the ministry of the apostles, healing does not seem to have played as prominent a role in the experience of the New Testament churches, at least as reflected in the epistles. Do, however, see James 5:14–16.

Jesus Frees Those Brought to Him (Matthew 8:16; Mark 1:32–34; Luke 4:40–41)

When evening came, many who were [demonized] were brought to him, and he drove out the spirits with a word and healed all the sick.

Matthew 8:16

This, rather than the experience in the synagogue, which we will discuss in a moment, is typical of Jesus' ministry to the demonized. Friends or neighbors or relatives were aware of something gone awry in a person's life. They then took the initiative to bring that person to Jesus.

"many who were [demonized]"—Demonization was not unusual in the time of Jesus; the text describes the demonized as "many." Although a number of Christians fail even to acknowledge the existence of demons, the chances are that many more in our society are influenced by evil spirits than we begin to imagine. Demonization is far more common than we think.

"were brought"—There seems to be no recorded case of a demonized person coming voluntarily to Jesus seeking deliverance, except possibly in the case of the demoniac of Gadara (see Mark 5:2).

We live in a society where symptoms of possible demonization are dismissed as mental aberrations or personality disorders. We take such persons to psychiatrists to be given medication. There is no doubt that at times this is appropriate. But friends and relatives need to consider the possibility of a demonic presence.

This reminds us that chapter 13 of this book, "Symptoms of Demonization," is an important one to master. We each need to be aware of the reality of evil spirits and of the ways in which they influence their victims. If we suspect a friend or loved one is demonized, we need to take the initiative in helping him or her.

When we cast out demons in Jesus' name, we are doing as these people did in Jesus' day. We are bringing the sufferer to the Lord and, as Jesus commanded demons in His days on earth, so He commands them today.

"to him"—Note that the people in first-century Galilee and Judea knew to whom the demonized could be brought.

Jesus had established a reputation as a healer and exorcist. It is a tragedy in our own day not only that demonization goes unrecognized, but that when demonization is suspected most of us have no idea where to turn. Yet any Christian, acting in Jesus' name, is authorized to cast out demons.

"he drove out the spirits with a word"—This stunned a people who imagined that the memorization of incantations and the performance of rituals were necessary when confronting the supernatural. Jesus simply commanded the demons to leave—something we, too, can do in Jesus' name.

The Demonized Man of Gadara (Matthew 8:28–34; Mark 5:1–20; Luke 8:26–39)

> Then Jesus asked him, "What is your name?"
> "My name is Legion," he replied, "for we are many."
>
> Mark 5:9

The familiar story of a man infested with a legion (thousands) of demons is related in all three of the synoptic gospels. And each gospel writer devotes an unusual amount of text to telling his story. The repetition of the story and the space devoted to it in each gospel indicate that this story is vital for our understanding of demonization. Much of what we can learn from the details in the three reports is developed in chapter 11 of this book.

There is more to be gained, however. Working from Mark 5, we can summarize some of these additional insights.

"What is your name?"—Mark depicts Jesus commanding, "Come out of this man, you evil spirit!" (Mark 5:8). Apparently the demons did not respond to this general command, leading Jesus to ask, "What is your name?"

Earlier I wrote about the importance of casting out demons by name. The significance of speaking to demons by name is underlined here. The point is not that Christ was unaware of the identities of the demons who were afflicting their victims. In biblical times, names had great significance. Names were not just labels, but revealed something of the nature or essence of the thing named. To be able to name something was believed to establish some level of control or influence over him or it. By stating their name, these demons acknowledged Christ's right to command them, and lost any ability to resist, as they had resisted His first command.

When casting out demons today, we need to be sure to find out the demons' names. We need to address them directly by name (see the discussion in chapter 14).

"The demons begged Jesus, 'Send us among the pigs; allow us to go into them' "—This peculiar request, reported in Mark 5:12, provides significant insight into the situation of demons. It suggests that demons are uncomfortable when not joined to some living creature, an idea confirmed by Jesus' remarks in Luke 11:24. The practical implication is that we should not simply command evil spirits to leave a demonized person. We also should not allow them to go to another living creature. Instead, we should send them to Jesus, for Him to dispose of as He chooses.

"Those who had seen it told the people what had happened to the [demonized] man—and told them about the pigs as well"—In Mark 5:16 we read that the people of the region reacted with awe and amazement when they saw the man, "sitting there, dressed and in his right mind." But an even greater impression seems to have been made by the report that the pigs the demons had entered all ran into the lake and

were drowned. The outcome was that "the people began to plead with Jesus to leave their region."

Do not expect people to praise you for casting out others' demons. Most will not want to have their normal way of thinking or living challenged by evidence either of the supernatural or of Jesus' power over evil spirits.

Connection to Illness (Matthew 9:32–33)

> While they were going out, a man who was [demonized] and could not talk was brought to Jesus. And when the demon was driven out, the man who had been mute spoke.
>
> Matthew 9:32–33

Here we see a clear connection between demonization and disability.

"when the demon was driven out, the man who had been mute spoke"—It was the demon's presence that precipitated the muteness, and when the demon was "driven out" the man could speak again.

In cases where an illness or disability has a spiritual rather than organic cause, we might very well see physical healing when we drive out demons. Yet demonized persons could also have organically caused illnesses. The symptoms of any illness might be exaggerated by demonization and be reduced after the demon is exorcised. But healing does not always follow when we cast out demons.

A False Charge (Matthew 9:34)

> But the Pharisees said, "It is by the prince of demons that [Jesus] drives out demons."
>
> Matthew 9:34

The Pharisees were highly respected by the Jews of Jesus' day for their commitment to the Law, but they felt threatened by Christ's popularity and saw Him as a rival.

"It is by the prince of demons that he drives out demons"— Since they could not deny the miracles Jesus performed, or that He was able to expel demons, the Pharisees charged that Christ's power over demons came from Satan rather than God. As this rumor spread and the charge was repeated, Jesus finally responded (see Matthew 12:22–32; Mark 3:20–30; Luke 11:14–23).

We can hardly be surprised if our understanding of demonization and our ministry of freeing the oppressed by driving out the demons is misunderstood or even attacked. Those committed to a theology that ignores or denies the role of the demonic in believers' lives have vested interests that might keep them from acknowledging what they witness.

Jesus Grants the Twelve Authority (Matthew 10:1–10; Mark 3:13–19; Luke 9:1–3)

> He called his twelve disciples to him and gave them authority to drive out evil spirits and to heal every disease and sickness.
>
> Matthew 10:1

In each of the passages that report this mission, Jesus told His disciples to take nothing with them. The disciples needed to rely on those to whom they ministered to supply their food and lodging. Their taking nothing emphasized their utter dependence on the Lord to provide, not only for their material needs but also for the "power and authority" (Luke 9:1) to drive out demons.

"gave them authority"—In these three passages only the twelve disciples were granted this unique authority. The Twelve are called *apostles* in Mark 3:14, a word that means "ones sent on a mission." And their mission was "to preach and to have authority to drive out demons." While we might conclude from Matthew 10, Mark 3 and Luke 9 that *only* the twelve apostles were given authority to expel demons, it is clear from Luke 10 that this authority was also extended to other followers of Jesus. (See the comments on Luke 10 in chapter 10, "Deliverance Ministry Ground Rules.")

Regarding healing, the passage in Mark 3 mentions only "authority to drive out demons." This does not mean that Jesus' disciples were unable to heal sicknesses, but it does suggest that "authority to drive out evil spirits" had priority.

"authority"—The Greek word here is *exousia*. This important term is found frequently in the New Testament and is typically translated "authority" or, a few times, "power." In every case, however, the underlying meaning of *exousia* is "freedom of choice." The greater one's authority, the greater the freedom he or she has to act in a certain area—and the greater the ability to limit others' freedom to act. In giving the disciples authority to drive out demons, Jesus was expanding His followers' freedom to command demons and was limiting the freedom of demons to resist their commands. The disciples were free to drive out the demons; the demons were no longer free to resist the disciples' commands.

"authority to drive out evil spirits"—Let's be clear about one thing. Although the apostles had authority over evil spirits, there were limits. The Twelve were free to "drive out" evil spirits, but they were *not* free to exercise any other kind of control over them.

There are times when people in deliverance ministry have ignored or misunderstood this limitation and tried to use demons as, for example, sources of information about the spirit realm. It was common in the ancient world to seek control of spirits in order to force or cajole them into harming a person's enemy, providing information about the future or ensuring economic or political success. Probably one of the most common motives was to force a desired man or woman to return one's love.

Because so many are tempted to misuse the authority Jesus gave us, I need to emphasize this point: Our authority over evil spirits is limited to driving them out of a person or a place that has been demonized. Any attempts to go beyond this significantly endanger us.

We have a great and wonderful authority to cast evil spirits out of a demonized individual. But that is the full extent of our authority over them.

The Charge Refuted (Matthew 12:22–32; Mark 3:20–30; Luke 11:14–23)

Then they brought him a [demonized] man who was blind and mute, and Jesus healed him, so that he could both talk and see. All the people were astonished and said, "Could this be the Son of David?" But when the Pharisees heard this, they said, "It is only by Beelzebub, the prince of demons, that this fellow drives out demons."

Jesus knew their thoughts and said to them, ". . . If I drive out demons by the Spirit of God, then the kingdom of God has come upon you. . . . Anyone who speaks a word against the Son of Man will be forgiven, but anyone who speaks against the Holy Spirit will not be forgiven."

Matthew 12:22–25, 28, 32

154

Matthew 9:34 introduces a strategy adopted by the religious leaders to undermine Jesus' approval by the people of Galilee and Judea. Their claim was that the miracles Jesus performed were energized by "the prince of demons" (here called *Beelzebub*) rather than energized by God. In these extended passages Jesus essentially ridicules this notion. There is a great deal that can be drawn from Jesus' argument, but I want to emphasize a few things from one line in particular: "If I drive out demons by the Spirit of God. . . ."

"If"—The Greek language has several different constructions that we translate "if." One of them indicates that the condition is assumed to be true. This is the construction used in this verse, so today we would probably say it like this: "Since I drive out demons by the Spirit of God. . . ." Jesus is clearly and unmistakably telling His audience that He actually does drive out demons by the Spirit of God.

"by the Spirit of God"—In the discussion of Jesus' temptations in part 2, I noted that Christ's response to Satan's first temptation was to quote a verse from Deuteronomy: "Man shall not live by bread alone." The emphasis in both testaments is placed on the word *man*. In essence, Jesus was telling Satan that He would meet each test in His humanity, not relying on resources available to Him as deity.

This is a critical verse and concept, and its interpretation is confirmed by Jesus' affirmation that He cast out demons and performed His other miracles by the Spirit of God. That is, Jesus was not speaking as God the Son when He drove out demons; rather, He was speaking as an authentic human being. It was Jesus, the child of Mary, a true human being, who cast out demons.

Why is this so important? Simply because if Jesus' authority to cast out demons derived from His deity, there is no way that we ordinary human beings could expect to cast out demons today. But Jesus did not cast out demons by His own power! Jesus cast out demons by the Spirit of God. And while Jesus is not present with us today, the Holy Spirit is present *in* us (see John 14:17; 1 Corinthians 12:13). When we exercise our authority to cast out demons in Jesus' name, the Holy Spirit is the One who enforces our command and drives the evil spirits out.

Like Jesus, we, too, "drive out demons by the Spirit of God." We have the authority. The Holy Spirit has the power.

"anyone who speaks against [blasphemes] the Holy Spirit will not be forgiven"—Matthew focuses our attention on Jesus' warning. Jesus was God in human flesh, and while the leaders' attacks on Him could be forgiven, His miracles were done in the power of the Holy Spirit. Thus, to depict the works of the Spirit as satanic was blasphemy. The fact is that even the religious leaders knew that Jesus was at the very least a "teacher who has come from God. For no one could perform the miraculous signs you are doing if God were not with him" (John 3:2). The leaders' unforgivable sin was knowingly, consciously, to portray the unmistakable works of the Holy Spirit through Jesus as satanic.

When an Evil Spirit Returns (Matthew 12:43–45; Luke 11:24–26)

"When an evil spirit comes out of a man, it goes through arid places seeking rest and does not find it. Then it says, 'I will return to the house I left.' When it arrives, it finds the house unoccupied, swept clean and put in order. Then it goes and takes with it seven other spirits more wicked than itself, and they go in and live there. And the final condition of that man is worse than the first. That is how it will be with this wicked generation."

Matthew 12:43–45

Jesus was speaking to the religious leaders who accused Him of performing His exorcisms through Satan's power. Christ's response was to explain what happens when demons are driven out. In Jesus' analogy, the image of the "house" represents a person in whom an evil spirit has taken up residence. While Jesus' analogy was spoken to warn His listeners of what lay ahead, the analogy provides unique insight into demonization.

"When an evil spirit comes out"—Whether the spirit is driven out or leaves voluntarily is not stated. Jesus simply pictures a demon who, for whatever reason, leaves a person who has been demonized.

"it goes through arid places seeking rest"—For demons, the disembodied state is like a parched and barren landscape. The demon explores it, looking for a comfortable place to rest, but the terrain seems arid and lifeless. Note that this description helps to explain why the Legion of demons infesting the man of Gadara begged Jesus to let them go into the nearby herd of pigs. The demons felt more at home in the pigs than in a disembodied state.

This demon, however, determines to return to his "house" (the body, the person) it left.

"it finds the house unoccupied, swept clean and put in order"—Jesus says that this "house" is now "unoccupied." The once-demonized person, freed from the influence of the evil spirit, has put his life in order. He has revised his priorities and is now living a far more moral and ordered life. What is more, he has gotten rid of the sins that once dominated

his life, having swept his life clean. It would appear that the person Jesus is speaking of has made a great effort to reform and has largely succeeded!

But all that the person accomplished was achieved by self-effort. The Holy Spirit, by whom Jesus cast out demons, simply is not present. With no divine presence in the person's life, he is on his own.

"Then it goes and takes with it seven other spirits more wicked than itself, and they go in and live there"—Because the man's life is "unoccupied" by God's presence, he is more vulnerable than ever. Mere moral reform can never protect us from evil spirits. Only when we are filled by God's Spirit have we any protection at all from evil spirits. When we are in intimate relationship with Jesus, when we have repented of and abandoned our sin, and when we are living a truly righteous life, evil spirits might try to sway us toward sin, but they will find no open door through which to enter our lives.

"And the final condition of that man is worse than the first"—In the context of the passage, Jesus' point is made in the last sentence: Jesus is drawing an analogy between the path taken by demons and the path taken by His opponents. Like the demonized man, His opponents are on a path that leads to a similar and terrible "final condition." Ultimately the religious leaders became wicked enough to crucify the Son of God.

The Case of the Canaanite Woman (Matthew 15:21–28; Mark 7:24–30)

A Canaanite woman from that vicinity came to him, crying out, "Lord, Son of David, have mercy on me! My daughter is suffering terribly from [demonization]." Jesus did not answer a word.

Matthew 15:22–23

The story is important theologically, for the event foreshadowed a day when all humanity would be invited into personal relationship with God through trust in Jesus.

"Jesus did not answer a word"—Jesus at first ignored this pagan woman's cries. Finally Jesus answered, telling her, "I was sent only to the lost sheep of Israel" (Matthew 15:24). As God's covenant people, Israel had an established relationship with God and a basis for expecting His blessing. But this Canaanite woman, like the entire pagan world at that time, had no claim on God's mercy.

"Woman, you have great faith! Your request is granted"—This response, given in Matthew 15:28, shows that, as the dialogue between Jesus and the woman ended, she showed remarkable trust in Jesus' ability to meet her need. Acknowledging her faith, Jesus granted her request, and her daughter was healed.

This experience also clarifies an important question in deliverance ministry: Should we offer freedom from demonization to believers only, or should we minister deliverance to the unsaved, as well? Jesus' answer seems to be that in His mercy God might free those who have enough trust in Him to seek His help, whether or not they have a personal relationship with Him.

Admittedly, having enough faith to seek help from a deliverance minister is not saving faith. That requires trust in Jesus as Savior. But experiencing deliverance in the name of

159

Jesus surely will nurture what little faith is there, and it might well bloom into saving faith.

Underneath it all is the fact that pagans, like Christians, can and do suffer terribly from demonization. And God is a God of mercy who cares deeply for those who do not yet know Jesus, as well as for believers. There is no way to justify withholding exorcism from anyone who seeks to be freed.

A Demonized Child (Matthew 17:14–21; Mark 9:14–29; Luke 9:37–42)

> A man in the crowd answered, "Teacher, I brought you my son, who is possessed by a spirit that has robbed him of speech. Whenever it seizes him, it throws him to the ground. He foams at the mouth, gnashes his teeth and becomes rigid. I asked your disciples to drive out the spirit, but they could not."
>
> Mark 9:17–18

Mark here provides a detailed description of possible physical symptoms of demonization. That word *possible* is important. Demonization has a wide range of symptoms, as we discussed in chapter 13, "Symptoms of Demonization." The boy in this story displays extreme physical symptoms—symptoms that also fit an epileptic seizure.

"I brought you my son"—The man's intent was to bring his son to Jesus. But when Christ was not present, the man asked Jesus' disciples to drive out the spirit. In this case, despite the authority the disciples had been given, they were unable to compel the demon to leave. At this point Jesus came on the scene: "When the spirit saw Jesus, it immediately threw the boy into a convulsion. He fell to the ground and rolled around, foaming at the mouth" (Mark 9:20).

Again we have a graphic description of how this evil spirit affected the man's son. While this is not typical, it does represent one possible manifestation of demonization. Many deliverance ministers will wisely order a demon not to harm the person as it leaves. Whether the manifestation is intended to frighten onlookers or is simply an indication of the spirits' hatred of humans is not stated.

When asked how long the boy had been like this, the father answered: "From [early] childhood. . . . It has often thrown him into fire or water to kill him" (Mark 9:21–22). The deep-seated hostility of denizens of the spirit world is clearly displayed in this demon's attempts to kill the youth whose body it inhabited. There are no "good" demonic spirits. Yet many in our culture try to contact "spirit guides" through occult means, and invite them into their lives.

"If you can do anything, take pity on us and help us"— Here, in Mark 9:22, we read that the harried father begged Jesus for help. Here the *if* suggests uncertainty. This *if* implies, "Perhaps You can, perhaps You can't." When assured that "everything is possible for him who believes," the man exclaimed, "I do believe; help me overcome my unbelief!" (Mark 9:23–24).

The important thing to remember as we approach any deliverance situation is that a successful exorcism does not depend on the faith of the person to be delivered. As human beings we often feel like this father, both believing and doubting at the same time. Let's remember that the critical element in faith is whom we believe in, not how confident we may feel at the moment.

As those ministering deliverance, we know that we can trust in Jesus, because He is totally trustworthy, and He truly "can do anything."

"You deaf and mute spirit," he said, *"I command you, come out of him and never enter him again"*—Mark 9:25 tells us that Jesus addressed the demon by name, commanded him to come out and added, "Never enter him again."

Evil spirits will often attempt to return to the person they have oppressed. It is important that we command spirits not to return. And it is also vitally important to equip a freed individual to resist any attempted return (see chapter 17, "Clearing the Way").

"The spirit shrieked, convulsed him violently and came out"—Some in deliverance ministry seem to encourage this kind of manifestation as described in Mark 9:26. Certainly such manifestations may enhance a deliverance minister's reputation. But it is far better, for the demonized person and for any witnesses, to forbid them. Demonic manifestations typically create fear in onlookers and even in the person freed. What we want people to take away is the conviction that, as evil as demons are, they are helpless when we confront them in Jesus' name.

"Why couldn't we drive it out?"—After Jesus had gone indoors, His disciples asked Him privately why they had failed. He replied, "This kind can come out only by prayer" (Mark 9:28–29). Please note that Jesus did not tell the disciples that their failure to drive out the evil spirit was due to their lack of faith. Instead He focused attention on the demon, telling them "this kind" can come out only by prayer.

The word translated "kind" is *genus*, and as used here suggests a type or order of demons. We do know that there are ranks among both angels and demons (see, for instance, Daniel 10:12–13). Apparently the child was demonized by a more powerful demon than most.

I take the phrase *by prayer* to indicate a focused and total reliance on God to act. It was far too easy for the disciples to focus on the authority Jesus had given them rather than remember that the power was God's alone and to rely completely on Him.

In driving out this spirit Jesus identified it as "you deaf and mute spirit." Jesus also simply said, "I command you, come out of him and never enter him again." It is helpful to contrast this report with Jesus' dealing with a man "who was deaf and could hardly talk" (see Mark 7:31–37).

Note first, in the latter case, the man's disability was apparently organic, and Jesus went about healing him in a very different way from His deliverance of the child. Second, when it comes to dealing with demons, we are to "command" in Jesus' name.

The Devil's Doom (Matthew 25:41)

"Then he will say to those on his left, 'Depart from me, you who are cursed, into the eternal fire prepared for the devil and his angels.' "

Matthew 25:41

This is one of several verses that help us identify evil spirits as angels who committed to Satan when he rebelled against God.

"eternal fire prepared"—This verse also reminds us that the Lord did not conceive of a hell of eternal fire in order to punish humans. Rather, God has done everything possible to deliver us from such a destiny by sending Jesus to make full payment for our sins on Calvary.

From the beginning God has revealed Himself to humankind in the Creation, in man's memory of and stories about

His works, in conscience, in Scripture and in His Son. Only those who fail to respond with faith to God's revelation of Himself will share the demons' fate—a fate chosen by their unbelief.

In the Synagogue (Mark 1:21–28; Luke 4:31–37)

Jesus went into the synagogue and began to teach. . . . Just then a man in their synagogue who was [demonized] cried out, "What do you want with us, Jesus of Nazareth? Have you come to destroy us? I know who you are—the Holy One of God."

"Be quiet!" said Jesus sternly. "Come out of him!" The evil spirit shook the man violently and came out of him with a shriek.

Mark 1:21, 23–26

We do not expect to find a demonized man sitting beside us in church, but this probably happens more often than we imagine. In this case, no one brought the man to Jesus, as the gospels testify was typical. Instead, the terrified demon, recognizing Jesus, blurted out a question.

"Have you come to destroy us?"—The Greek word is *apollymai*, one of several translated "destroy." Their meanings include "to render unrecognizable, to tear down, to corrupt, to abolish or nullify and to undo." *Apollymai*, depending on context, is most often translated "destroy, perish, kill or put an end to." The demon was aware that Jesus is destined to send him to the lake of fire (see Matthew 25:41) but was unclear whether or not Christ's presence marked the time of his destruction.

It is encouraging when we confront demons to remember that they know their fate very well and know that they must submit to Jesus. They must also submit to us as we drive them out in Jesus' name.

"The evil spirit shook the man violently and came out of him with a shriek"—How do we explain the fact that at times demons went quietly, and at others, as on this occasion, their departure was clearly marked? One possible reason is that in the early days of Jesus' ministry, as here in Mark 1, Jesus was establishing His identity as God's messenger. It is no wonder that Nicodemus, a member of the Sanhedrin, admitted, "We know you are a teacher who has come from God. For no one could perform the miraculous signs you are doing if God were not with him" (John 3:2). Manifestations by the demons, like the physical healings Jesus performed, convinced even the religious leaders who later demanded His crucifixion . . . despite what they knew.

"What is this teaching? With authority and power he gives orders to evil spirits and they come out!"—Here in Luke 4:36 we see Luke's report of the reaction of other people in the synagogue to Jesus' actions.

The word translated "teaching" here is *logos*. It is generally translated "word," but it has many complex meanings in both Greek philosophical writings and in Scripture. What the observers are asking is not "What is this teaching?" but "What is the significance of, or the message in, what we are seeing and hearing?" Jesus was giving orders to evil spirits who obeyed Him, showing that Jesus had both authority and power.

The answer to the question, of course, is that Jesus is the promised Messiah, God come to be with us, as Isaiah predicted. Yet despite the obvious evidence presented in Jesus' actions, the crowds hesitated to trust Him, and the religious leaders felt their position so threatened that they decided to kill Him.

Demons See His Glory (Mark 3:11–12)

> Whenever the evil spirits saw him, they fell down before him and cried out, "You are the Son of God." But he gave them strict orders not to tell who he was.
>
> Mark 3:11–12

"Whenever the evil spirits saw him"—In Mark's depictions of Jesus' confrontations with demons, they seemed compelled to acclaim Him loudly as the Son of God. It is not that the demons recognized Him and were glad to see Him. Instead, they were compelled to fall down before Him and acclaim Him simply because they could see Him as He is.

"But he gave them strict orders not to tell who he was"—We read in a number of passages that Jesus silenced demons when He encountered them, unwilling to accept their testimony. He did not allow demons to tell who He was; the people of Israel would have to watch and listen to Him, and make their own decisions. The silencing theme is repeated in these verses.

Philippians reminds us that the day is coming when, "at the name of Jesus every knee should bow, in heaven and on hearth and under the earth, and every tongue confess that Jesus Christ is Lord" (Philippians 2:10–11). This day is fast approaching when every living being—humans, angels and demons alike—will bow and confess that Jesus is Lord. The glory that the demons sensed in Jesus will be fully revealed at His Second Coming, and those of us who love Him will praise Him gladly, while those who do not will be compelled to recognize the Lord as the one they rejected.

The Man Driving Out Demons (Mark 9:38-41; Luke 9:49–50)

> "Teacher," said John, "we saw a man driving out demons in your name and we told him to stop, because he was not one of us."
>
> Mark 9:38

The Twelve were thrilled by the authority they were given to drive out demons. It, as well as their positions as disciples and constant companions of Jesus, seemed to set them apart. Then they saw "a man" driving out demons in Jesus' name.

"we saw a man driving out demons in your name"—It is not surprising they told the man to stop. Since he was not one of the inner circle, his success in driving out demons threatened their uniqueness.

But it is clear from the fact that the man was freeing people from evil spirits in Jesus' name that he honored and trusted in Jesus, even though he was not one of the Twelve. I suspect the disciples expected Jesus to praise them for their actions. Instead, He told them they were wrong. Certainly a person who had just cast out demons in Jesus' name could not "in the next moment say anything bad about" Him (Mark 9:39).

We need to avoid the attitude displayed here by the disciples. What sets believers apart from the world is not our membership in a group or denomination. It is not our theological stance, or even ordination. What sets us apart is our trust in Jesus, and this alone qualifies us to act in His name.

Mary Magdalene (Mark 16:9)

> When Jesus rose early on the first day of the week, he appeared first to Mary Magdalene, out of whom he had driven seven demons.
>
> Mark 16:9

The text makes it clear that Mary was the first to see the risen Christ, and also the first to give witness to others of His resurrection (see Mark 16:10).

"he appeared first to Mary Magdalene"—This choice by God was striking on two accounts. In first-century Jewish courts, women were deemed unreliable and were not allowed to give testimony of any kind. And Mary had not only been demonized, but Mark's comment about the seven demons tells us that her demonization was well-known. Despite her sex and her previous oppression by demons, God chose Mary for this very special role.

What a comfort to those from whom demons have been driven! Any previous oppression by evil spirits in no way disqualifies a delivered person from a significant role in the service of God.

Accompanying Signs (Mark 16:14–20)

"And these signs will accompany those who believe: In my name they will drive out demons; they will speak in new tongues; they will pick up snakes with their hands; and when they drink deadly poison, it will not hurt them at all; they will place their hands on sick people, and they will get well."

Mark 16:17–18

Mark 16:9–20 is not found in the earliest manuscripts of Mark's gospel. Some believe these verses were added later; others argue they were part of the original text.

"these signs will accompany those who believe"—What we can say for sure is that exorcisms were not uncommon in the early Church, that Paul for one was bitten by a deadly viper (see Acts 28:3–6), and that the disciples did "place their

hands on sick people" who were then healed (Acts 28:8–10). It is also true that placing hands on a person for healing is not reported in any other passage in Acts or the epistles. In both Testaments this practice is linked only to the commissioning of a person for some role or special ministry.

The Source of Power (Luke 6:18–19)

> Those troubled by evil spirits were cured, and the people all tried to touch him, because power was coming from him and healing them all.
>
> Luke 6:18–19

The Old Testament looks back on the miracles performed by God to free Israel from Egypt as the defining exercise of God's power. The New Testament looks to the resurrection of Jesus as the defining exercise. That "incomparably great power" (Ephesians 1:19) is life-giving and transforming. It overwhelms demons and sickness.

"power was coming from him"—The Greek word translated "power" here is *dynamis*. Luke describes how the recognition of Jesus' power impelled people to draw close and try to touch Him. Jesus was the source of transforming power then, and He is the source of transforming power now. No wonder we drive out demons in His name!

No Doubts Now (Luke 7:18–23)

> "John the Baptist sent us to you to ask, 'Are you the one who was to come, or should we expect someone else?'"
> At that very time Jesus cured many who had diseases, sicknesses and evil spirits, and gave sight to many who were

blind. So he replied to the messengers, "Go back and report to John what you have seen and heard: The blind receive sight, the lame walk, those who have leprosy are cured, the deaf hear, the dead are raised, and the good news is preached to the poor."

Luke 7:20–22

The Old Testament portrays the coming Messiah as a mighty king and worldwide ruler, who would restore Israel to prominence among the nations. But Jesus showed no inclination to proclaim Himself the Messiah or drive Rome from history's stage.

"Are you the one who was to come . . . ?"—Even John the Baptist could not reconcile this seeming failure with his early conviction that Jesus was the Messiah. Luke describes what happened when John sent some of his disciples to ask Jesus if He truly was "the one." Jesus did not respond in words. Instead, He exercised His power to heal and to free from demonic oppression. Jesus then paraphrased Isaiah 35:5–6, which associates miraculous healings with the day "your God will come" (Isaiah 35:4).

While the healings and freeing from demonic oppression were primarily rooted in God's concern for human beings, they also were evidence pointing to Jesus' identity as the promised Messiah. Today when we drive out demons, we need to be sure that our actions point to and glorify Jesus, rather than enhance our personal reputations.

The Seventy-Two (Luke 10:1–24)

The seventy-two returned with joy and said, "Lord, even the demons submit to us in your name."

He replied, "I saw Satan fall like lightning from heaven. I have given you authority to trample on snakes and scorpions and to overcome all the power of the enemy; nothing will harm you. However, do not rejoice that the spirits submit to you, but rejoice that your names are written in heaven."

Luke 10:17–20

A number of things in this lengthy passage have special meaning as we consider deliverance ministry.

"Lord, even the demons submit to us in your name"— Other passages in the gospels that tell of Jesus' gift of authority to drive out demons identify the twelve disciples explicitly as recipients of this authority. Yet in this passage 72 "others" were sent on a preaching tour. While Jesus gave them clear instructions on how to go about their mission, and told them to "heal the sick" as well as announce that the Kingdom of God was near, the text does not record the giving of specific authority to expel demons. But when the 72 returned they were thrilled that even the demons submitted to them in His name.

Two things are especially significant about this report. First, the 72 were not disciples. They were "others," nameless followers of Jesus. Obviously it was not necessary to be one of the twelve disciples either to share the Good News about Jesus or to drive out demons.

This is important, for (1) it sets to rest the false notion that only the Twelve were given this authority, and (2) it also sets to rest the notion that Christ had to explicitly extend authority over demons for that authority to exist. Now, as then, neither ordination nor an express commission is necessary to share the Gospel or to drive out demons. As "others" who follow Jesus, we all have the authority we need to expel evil spirits from a demonized individual.

"The seventy-two returned with joy"—It seems that the 72 were thrilled and impressed by the fact that demons submitted to them in Jesus' name. We can understand how special this seemed to them. We can even understand why they focused on their unexpected power over evil spirits. Yet it seems strange that this experience dominated their thinking. There is no report here of the responses of villagers where the Word was welcomed, no excitement over those who welcomed them in the Savior's name. The 72 seem to have been entirely focused on their newfound power over demons.

"Rejoice that your names are written in heaven"—Jesus' response to the report is a rebuke. Jesus almost dismissed their report with the remark that He Himself had seen "Satan fall like lightning from heaven." It was true that they now had authority "to overcome all the power of the enemy." But what they should rejoice in was the fact "that your names are written in heaven."

As strange as it seemed to the 72, and as strange as it may seem to us today, authority to drive out demons is not that wonderful a thing. And exorcising evil spirits is not that great an accomplishment. Satan is a defeated enemy, and his hosts of demons are on the losing, not the winning, side. What is wonderful is that through trust in Jesus our names are written in heaven.

We need to be careful to maintain balance when it comes to deliverance ministry. Yes, it is a privilege to drive evil spirits out of those who are oppressed. But the important thing is the Gospel itself, and what Jesus has done for sinners who are alienated from God. Let's not glorify those who drive out demons—or become puffed up when we do it ourselves. Let's rejoice in the salvation Jesus has won for us, and that through us He offers this gift to all humankind.

A Crippled Woman Healed (Luke 13:10–17)

A woman was there who had been crippled by a spirit for eighteen years. She was bent over and could not straighten up at all.

Luke 13:11

This story should help to correct those who think that believers are immune to demonization. This was not the case in the Old Testament era, nor is it the case in the Church Age.

"crippled by a spirit"—There is no doubt that physical illness or disability may be exacerbated by demons. This does not mean that all, or even that most, health problems have a demonic origin. But certainly some do, and when a disability is chronic and does not respond to medical treatment or to psychological counseling, we do need to consider seriously the possibility of demonization.

"Woman, you are set free from your infirmity"—In this case, as described in Luke 13:12, Jesus did not explicitly drive out the demon. He simply announced that the woman was set free from the crippling presence.

"this woman, a daughter of Abraham"—The president of the synagogue was upset because Jesus had healed the woman on the Sabbath, something he regarded as work, which was forbidden on the Sabbath. Jesus not only rebuked him for his heartlessness but also identified the woman as "a daughter of Abraham" (Luke 13:16). The phrase is important, because it indicates more than physical descent from Abraham and Sarah. To be called a daughter of Abraham indicated that the woman had a special, personal relationship with God,

based on the kind of trust that Abraham had in the Lord (see Romans 4:16–25).

Jesus Is Accused of Demonization (John 7:19–20)

"Has not Moses given you the law? Yet not one of you keeps the law. Why are you trying to kill me?"
"You are [demonized]," the crowd answered. "Who is trying to kill you?"

John 7:20

In other situations where Jesus was accused of association with demons, the Pharisees were the accusers, and they were trying desperately to explain away the miracles of healing Jesus performed. In this case, "the crowd" was making the accusation. And their charge was not a reaction to His miracles, but to His statement that "you [are] trying to kill me."

"*You are [demonized]*"—The charge the crowd made is equivalent to saying, "You're crazy." The crowd ridiculed Jesus by saying that He was out of His mind, as some demonized persons were. His thinking and understanding were distorted. No one was trying to kill Him.

While the incident provides some insight into mental symptoms of demonization, it provides more insight into the state of mind of the people of Jerusalem. As John 7:25 shows, "some of the people of Jerusalem began to ask, 'Isn't this the man they are trying to kill? Here he is, speaking publicly, and they are not saying a word to him.'" The authorities then tried to arrest and silence Jesus, but the Temple guards refused to carry out the orders (see John 7:45–46).

All too soon events would prove that Jesus was hardly confused about the intent of the religious authorities.

Satan: The Father of Lies (John 8:31–47)

To the Jews who had believed him, Jesus said, "If you hold to my teaching, you are really my disciples. Then you will know the truth, and the truth will set you free." They answered him, "We are Abraham's descendants and have never been slaves of anyone. How can you say that we shall be set free?"

John 8:31–33

Here Jesus introduced another aspect of Satan's work. While it does not involve the demonization of individuals as such, it does depict a satanic strategy that we might call the demonization of our race.

"Abraham's descendants"—Israel's religion was rooted in covenant promises God made to Abraham and his descendants. While the promises established the Jews as a covenant people, having a unique relationship with God, salvation of individual Jews depended on personal trust in God like that of Abraham (see Genesis 15:6). Missing this truth, most first-century Jews believed that God "owed" Abraham so much for responding to His call that Abraham's excess merits could be and were credited to his descendants. The excess merits, plus a person's own good deeds, would win him or her a place in the future life. Thus, the claim here to be "Abraham's descendants" was a claim to an established relationship with God.

"have never been slaves of anyone"—This claim was patently false. At that very moment the Jews were dominated by Rome, which taxed them unmercifully and stationed armies in Judea and Galilee to enforce obedience. But Jesus had another kind of slavery in mind. He pointed out that, like all

of humankind, the Jews were slaves to sin and desperately needed to be set free.

"I know you are Abraham's descendants"—In John 8:37, we read Jesus' acknowledgment that His listeners were biological descendants of Abraham. But the question was, Were they spiritual descendants of Abraham?

"Yet you are ready to kill me, because you have no room for my word. . . . You are doing the things your own father does"—These comments, given in John 8:37, 41, show their reaction to Jesus. Both the deep-seated hostility to Him personally and their rejection of His Word made it very clear that their real relationship was not with God but with another "father." Here, *father* is used in the sense of source or originator. In Jewish thought God had established the covenant community, and in that limited sense was their father. Jesus, however, in claiming God as His Father, affirmed both a unique personal relationship with God and also equality with God.

" 'We are not illegitimate children,' they protested"—The reaction to Jesus' statements was angry denial, and an unfounded claim that "the only Father we have is God himself" (John 8:41). Christ's response was blunt: "If God were your Father, you would love me" (verse 42). Jesus then goes even further.

"You belong to your father, the devil"—The root and source of the listeners' response was Satan himself. These people chose to believe a lie and rejected the truth Jesus was presenting. In this they showed they were related to Satan, and bore the family resemblance. Jesus continued, "For he is a liar and the father of lies" (John 8:44).

Later John will quote Jesus' claim: "I am the way and the truth and the life" (John 14:6). All who react against the truth, and who believe lies about themselves and their standing with God, are choosing to stand with Satan rather than with God and His Christ. Whether or not they are the victims of individual demons, they have been powerfully influenced by Satan. And they have chosen his way.

The Choice (John 10:19–21)

Many of them said, "He is [demonized] and raving mad. Why listen to him?" But others said, "These are not the sayings of a man possessed by a demon. Can a demon open the eyes of the blind?"

John 10:19–21

Again it is Jesus' presentation of Himself, this time as the Good Shepherd who lays down His life for His sheep, that crystallizes intense debate.

"'He is [demonized]. . . .' But others said, . . . 'Can a demon open the eyes of the blind?'"—Those who rejected Him insisted that His teaching was the ranting of a madman in the grip of a demon. But others saw that Jesus stated His claims clearly and rationally. It was obvious that what Jesus said was not the confused ranting of a demonized individual. Those on this side of the debate also pointed to a miracle Jesus had performed earlier. It was firmly believed by the Jews that only God could be the source of such miracles.

Again we see one of the symptoms of demonization: confused, and even raving, speech and thought. And again we see how strongly the evidence supported Jesus' claims of who He was. We better see what Paul means when he writes in

2 Corinthians 4:4 that the "god of this age [Satan] has blinded the minds of unbelievers, so that they cannot see the light of the gospel of the glory of Christ."

The Devil's Prompting (John 13:2)

> The evening meal was being served, and the devil had already prompted Judas Iscariot, son of Simon, to betray Jesus.
>
> John 13:2

John tells us that Satan's purpose (occurring before this night of the Last Supper) was to "prompt" Judas to make an agreement with the chief priests to betray Jesus.

"The devil had already prompted Judas"—Luke tells when this prompting took place: The Passover feast "was approaching, and the chief priests and the teachers of the law were looking for some way to get rid of Jesus. . . . Then Satan entered Judas" and he went to them (Luke 22:1–3). Judas then bargained with the chief priests to betray Jesus for thirty pieces of silver (see Matthew 26:14–15). Satan, from his position in Judas, "prompted" Judas to betray Jesus. Many believe such prompting involves planting ideas in the demonized person's mind.

In the Greek, a four-word phrase occurs where the translators chose to use *prompt*. The Greek tells us, literally, that Satan "threw into the heart" of Judas the idea to betray Jesus. The imagery helps us to avoid a significant error. Satan did not cause, force or make Judas willing to betray the Lord. He threw out the idea, and Judas caught it!

It is clear that the choice to betray the Lord was Judas' alone. Satan was eager for Judas to betray Christ to the religious leaders, who were intent on killing Christ. But Judas alone was responsible for making the fatal choice.

Satan Enters Judas (John 13:26–30)

Then, dipping the piece of bread, [Jesus] gave it to Judas
Iscariot, son of Simon. As soon as Judas took the bread,
Satan entered into him. . . . As soon as Judas had taken the
bread, he went out. And it was night.

John 13:26–27, 30

John is very clear about the sequence of events on Jesus' last
night on earth. He notes, as we read above, that Satan had
"thrown into the heart" of Judas the idea to betray Jesus (see
John 13:2). This had happened "already," before the Last
Supper began.

"Satan entered into him"—We know from the references in
the gospels to "driving out" evil spirits that they were, in some
sense, "in" the demonized individual. What we do not know is
exactly what it means for a demon to be "in" a human being.
Here we are told that during the supper, Satan "entered" Judas.
The Greek word for *entered* here is *eiserchomai*, and is a common word used of entering a building or going into a house.

"Judas left"—Why Satan was eager to be present personally when Judas actually did betray Jesus is a matter of specu-
lation. Perhaps he felt a need to strengthen Judas' resolve,
or perhaps he simply wanted to witness close up what he
expected to be Jesus' defeat.

But however strong Satan's influence "in" Judas, Satan's
presence does not imply that the evil one took over the body
of Judas and acted independently. Judas remained responsible
for the bargain he made with the chief priests and for his
subsequent betrayal of Jesus.

Since demons can and do influence the choices of those
they inhabit, it is especially important that we be alert to

drive them out. This is also why it is important in deliverance ministry to gain the cooperation and consent of a demonized individual before we drive out the demon(s). It is possible that the person actually welcomes the presence of the demons and chooses to keep them. Even if we should drive the demons out, such a person will all too soon welcome them back again.

Conclusion

It would almost seem that Satan triumphed here, for Judas' betrayal, encouraged by Satan, led to the crucifixion of the Savior. But the apostle Paul sees the events very differently. Yes, Satan and his fellow demons were intent on killing the Son of God. But Paul, writing of the wisdom of God, critiques the "wisdom of this age [and] of the rulers of this age" (1 Corinthians 2:6). Again, remember by *rulers* Paul is pointing to evil spirits who are intent on establishing Satan's kingdom. Paul writes of God's wisdom that "none of the rulers of this age understood it, for if they had, they would not have crucified the Lord of glory" (1 Corinthians 2:8). In the wisdom of God, the Savior's death led to resurrection and the salvation of all who believe.

Satan intends to destroy us all. But the Lord of glory is the Lord of resurrection. Even the best laid of Satan's plans, and the fiercest of his attacks, will fall before the wisdom of our God and the authority He has given us to conduct spiritual warfare Jesus' way.

Index

Larry Richards holds a B.A. in philosophy from the University of Michigan, a Th.M. in Christian education from Dallas Theological Seminary and a Ph.D. in religious education and social psychology from Garrett Biblical Seminary and Northwestern University jointly. He has taught in the Wheaton College Graduate School, served as a minister of Christian education and written more than two hundred books, including theological works, commentaries and several specialty and study Bibles. Larry is currently a full-time author and speaker. He and his wife, Sue, live in Raleigh, North Carolina.

More Wisdom From Larry Richards

Stand firm against the devil's schemes with this ironclad, hands-on defense plan straight from the Bible. Using Paul's letter to the Ephesians as his infallible guide, Richards reveals how God provides protection from every attack of the enemy—and how you can put on the full armor of God today and every day.

The Full Armor of God

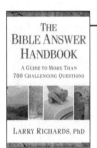

Find biblical answers to over 700 questions about the Bible in this fascinating resource. Working through the Bible book by book, Richards looks at a wide range of perplexing questions on topics ranging from authorship and internal contradictions to historical inaccuracy. He also sheds light on the meaning and implications of hard-to-understand passages, while always maintaining the view that the Bible is reliable and trustworthy.

The Bible Answer Handbook

✓Chosen

10/14